Martin Heidegger
A Study in Existential Philosophy

Der eine
Fremdsprache nicht kennt kennt nichts von seiner eigenen
(He who does not know a foreign language will not know nothing of himself.)

Johann Wolfgang von Goethe (1749-1832)

Martin Heidegger
A Study in Existential Philosophy

Hamsa Arniker

Prestige Books International

New Delhi : Sydney

Published by
Prestige Books International
New Delhi 110 060
email: prestigebooks@gmail.com

Associate Office
60/29-45 Parramatta Road,
Concord, NSW 2137
Australia

ISBN: 978-93-82185-25-0

Printed in India

Contents

Dedicated with Shradda and Bhakti

to

Mallampalli Sarabheswara Sarma (1928-2007)

popularly known as Sarabhayya

a renowned Indian poet, critic, translator and

a great exponent of classical literature

Preface

The present work is an attempt at an exposition of Martin Heidegger's thought as contained in his seminal work, *Being and Time*. It presents a detailed study of Heidegger's conception of Dasein, the central theme of the earlier phase of his philosophical career. It is my acquaintance with German language that motivated me to undertake research into Heidegger's philosophy. Reading *Sein und Zeit* in German with the help of its English translation fascinated me. It helped me in getting to know Heidegger's thought more deeply and passionately. Given the limited scope of the present research, several other works relating to the later phase of Heidegger's thought had to be left out. In presenting Heidegger's phenomenological ontology of human existence and the meaning of Being, I have tried to be as systematic and comprehensive as possible. More importantly, I have also tried to be faithful to the original text of *Being and Time*. I hope this book will be of some use to the teachers and students of Philosophy, and to all those who are interested in Heidegger in general.

I cannot close this prefatory note without expressing my gratitude to all those who rendered help and cooperation in the preparation of this project. I am grateful to my husband, Dr. G. Vedaparayana, Professor Emeritus, presently Senior Fellow, I.C.P.R. Department of Philosophy, S.V. University, Tirupati, for being a friend, philosopher and guide. I thank my parents, brother, sister and my daughters—Amrita Vedaparayana and Ahalya Vedaparayana—for their motivation and affection during the entire course of my study.

Teachers are the fountain-head of inspiration. I particularly express my gratitude to German Language faculty— Herr. Rajan, my teacher, in Max Muller Bhavan, Hyderabad (1980), Dr. Lucia Igel (former East Germany), who was my teacher in my third-year Advanced Diploma in German at Osmania University (1988). Further I am deeply beholden to Dr. Regina Muhlenweg (former West Germany), Sri. V.S Sharma of Chennai Max Mueller Bhavan, Prof. Majan Mulla of Karnatak University, Dharwad, and Prof. Somanci Krishna Sarma and Prof. T. Asoka Rani to have magnanimously provided me with some invaluable books, most of these from their personal collections, without which it would not have been possible to gain command over the source language and execute this into a project, with the unstinted support from my husband who took pains and taught me the rudiments of various methods and systems of Western Philosophy. My modest assignment as a part-time English teacher in SPMVV (Women's University) and Rashtriya Sanskrit Vidyapeetha in Tirupati, all these years, helped me sustain and devote long hours to my academic pursuits.

My grateful thanks to Prestige Books International, New Delhi, for publishing this book so expeditiously and elegantly. I am especially indebted to Dr. R.K. Dhawan and Dr. Suman Bala of the University of Delhi for their scholarly suggestions and meticulous editing and to Ms. D. Renu for overseeing the production of the book.

And finally, I thank all those who have contributed directly or indirectly in the successful completion of this project.

Chapter I

Introduction

A. Biography

Martin Heidegger (1889-1976) is one of the most profound and influential thinkers of the West. He is the central figure representing the phenomenological and existential movement in the twentieth century. His appeal and impact are so strong and wide that neither specialists nor beginners in philosophy can afford to be indifferent to his thought. Widely acclaimed as the philosopher of the contemporary times, Heidegger's influence cuts across the barriers of time and distance, culture and language. He has left an indelible impression on almost all the spheres of philosophical edifice.

Born in a farmer's family in a Schwabian village, Baden, in South Germany, Heidegger had a humble origin and lived in the simplicity of the natural environment. In 1915 he became a *Privatdozent* at the University of Freiburg and was trained in the phenomenological method of Edmund Husserl. He became Professor at Marburg in 1923, and at Freiburg in 1928. In 1933, he became the first National Socialist rector of the University of Freiburg. During this time, he publicly renounced his allegiance to Husserl's thought (which he however reinstated in his later works) and developed a strand of extreme sense of nationalism. In a public lecture, 'Role of the University in the New Reich,' Heidegger celebrated the advent of a glorious new Germany. He described Germans as the people of the centre, caught between the giant pincers of the two barbarian mass societies, Russia and America. He summoned his people to renew, as they alone can, the great 'beginning' of the Western thought and save humanity from nihilism and gadgetry. He appealed to them to save Being itself from mist and vapour man's history had made of it. Holding as he does a mystical view of language, Heidegger also subscribed with zeal to the widespread opinion that philosophizing is possible only in German and Greek. He regarded Greek as a holy language and German as a pure one. However, it is wrong to assess his thought in terms of his ideas of politics and nationalism. The depth of his thought ranging from theology to psychoanalysis, from metaphysics to environment, surpasses his national and political enthusiasm. Mostly living in the province of his origin, and often retiring to his mountain-hut, Heidegger always thought the same simple thought of Being by constantly asking the all-important question—what is it, to be? His sole aim had been to warn us of our failure to raise the question of Being which is our nature and responsibility. His mission was to summon us to our true vocation of answering the question of Being. He firmly believed that proper answer to the question of the meaning of Being would determine the fate of this earth and our existence on it. The eighty-seven long years of Heidegger's intellectually fertile, quiet and largely uneventful life and thought may be summed up in a sentence of his funeral oration by Bernard Welte: "He was always a seeker, and was always on the way."

B. Philosophy

Heidegger's philosophy is a consistent critique of the epistemological character of Western philosophy. It is an attack on the deteriorating Western metaphysical thinking founded on the theology, religion and culture of the West. As against the two millennia long monolithic Western philosophical tradition, Heidegger's philosophy is a clarion call to primordial thinking centred round fundamental ontology. His thought is a way-making movement of an authentic thinking of Being (*Sein*). It is the way of Being rather than the way towards Being. The 'way' of Being shows itself in being trodden upon in authentic thinking. The whole of Heidegger's philosophical enterprise is nothing but to be ever on the way of Being.

Investigation into the question of the meaning of Being is the central theme of Heidegger's philosophy. He begins his magnum opus, *Being and Time*, by deploring that the fundamental question, namely, the question of the meaning of Being has not been given a serious attention. The question of the meaning of Being has been almost forgotten and has come to seem as nothing. Humanity has fallen out of Being and lost the nearness and shelter of Being by foolishly running after this and that trivial thought. We have betrayed our true vocation which is to seek the ground, the Holy, namely, Being through which everything manifests. We live in a world darkened by our forgetfulness of what Being is and what we are. Our history is our forgetfulness and betrayal of Being and ourselves.

What has so far been unravelled about the meaning of Being is fragmentary. In the history of Western thought, the question of Being has been trivialized after Plato and Aristotle who made initial contributions to its interpretation. Although the question of Being persisted in different ways down to the logic of Hegel, incisive investigation into it has never taken place. The presuppositions that Being is the most universal, self-evident and indefinable concept have been a barrier to discovering a proper answer to the question of the meaning of Being. These assumptions have rendered the question obscure and without proper direction. Heidegger says that the question of the meaning of Being must be properly formulated and explained from the standpoint which can render it as a very special and distinctive question. Being should be faced with the infinite powers of man. Heidegger says that the very verb 'is' is a testimony to our understanding of Being. But the understanding of Being at this level is only vague, average and fluctuating. We cannot conceptually fix the horizon of the meaning of Being at this stage. Nevertheless, the very indefiniteness of Being is still a fact which needs to be clarified and developed into a concept.

Being is neither a genus nor a class. Its universality is beyond all categories and has to be sought beyond all entities. Yet Being is that which determines entities as entities and it is on the basis of Being that entities are already understood. Although Being refers to the 'isness' of the entities, Being is not itself an entity. Since Being is essentially different from the entities, Being has to be discovered and conceived in a way which is essentially different from the way the entities are discovered and conceived. There are many things which we designate as Being. We encounter Being in everything we have in view. Being is revealed in what we are and how we are. Being lies in the fact that something 'is.' It lies in reality and in Dasein as well. Of all the entities, Dasein is the only entity which has a genuine access to Being, for it alone is capable of understanding and conceiving. Dasein alone has the privilege of being the inquirer into Being. It has priority over all other entities in having access to Being. The question of the meaning of Being can be properly formulated and made transparent only by making Dasein as the starting point of inquiry. And it is only by choosing Dasein as the inquirer that Being can be elucidated properly.

The term "Dasein" ordinarily means existence in general. But Heidegger uses it in the specific sense of human existence. The term is composed of "Da" and "*Sein*" which respectively mean "there" and "being." The term thus means "being-there." It specially refers to man's conscious and historical existence which is always projected into a *there* beyond its *here.* Dasein is none other than human reality. Dasein is ourselves who are the inquirers into Being. Man is Dasein in so far as he is the "Da" of "*Sein.*" Besides being a synonym of Man, the term "Dasein" has a unique ontological significance. Heideggerian scholars use it untranslated in order to preserve its ontological meaning. Dasein is the entity which has a three-fold priority to inquiry into the question of Being. The three priorities are ontical, ontological and ontico-ontological. Since Dasein is ontically a distinct entity, it has an ontical priority to the question of Being. Dasein is ontically distinguished since in its Being, its Being is always in question for it. It is not an entity which simply occurs along with other entities. In it, Being is always in question which constitutes Dasein's Being. This is how Dasein has an access to Being through which it understands itself. In being ontically distinctive, Dasein also possesses an ontological character of theoretical inquiry into the meaning of entities. Thus Dasein has not only an ontical but also an ontological priority to the question of Being. Besides, the ontical and ontological priority, Dasein has an intico-ontological priority to the question of Being, since it possesses an understanding of its own Being as well as the Being of the entities which are different from it.

Thus Dasein is the only entity which must be questioned and analyzed ontologically for interpreting the meaning of Being in plain and transparent terms. Dasein alone can make possible the fundamental ontology which deals with the question of Being. It is through an existential analytic of Dasein that the fundamental ontology of Being must be worked out. The analytic of Dasein must not be dogmatic or arbitrary. It should be such that it allows Dasein to show itself in itself and from itself. That is, the interpretation should explicate Dasein in its essential structures which determine the character of its Being. It should be such that it reveals Dasein as Being-in-the-world and in its everydayness. The ontological analytic has to interpret Care, death and authenticity as the ownmost possibilities of Dasein. It has to demonstrate temporality as the meaning of the Being of Dasein. That is, Being has to be conceived and interpreted with time as the standpoint and horizon. The meanings of the modes and characteristics of Being must be determined in terms of time. That is, the fundamental ontology of interpreting Being should include working out the temporality of Being.

Phenomenology is the method that Heidegger adopts for the conception and interpretation of Being through the being of Dasein. Phenomenology is rooted in the way we come to terms with the things themselves. As the science of phenomenon, phenomenology may be formulated as 'to the things themselves.' It is a device of bringing phenomenon to the light of day by showing it out to be in itself and from itself. It is a discourse in which phenomenon is seen as something and in its togetherness with some other things. Phenomenology is letting phenomenon be seen from itself in the very way in which it shows itself from itself. It is grasping phenomenon in such a way that everything about it is demonstrated directly. It is a description of an object or an entity by establishing it in terms of its thinghood. It is a method of grasping phenomenon thematically and in terms of its ownmost content as a thing. Phenomenology therefore is a means of access to what is to be the theme of ontology. It is only as phenomenology that ontology is possible. Phenomenology and ontology are not two distinct disciplines. They together constitute a philosophy having phenomena as its object and its own way of treating it. In this sense philosophy itself is a universal phenomenological ontology which takes analysis of Dasein as its point of departure. As ontology phenomenology takes Dasein as its theme, since Dasein also is ontologically and ontically a distinctive entity. It is only by taking Dasein as its theme that phenomenology can confront the question of the meaning of Being in general. Phenomenological ontology, according to Heidegger, is hermeneutical in its primordial sense. That is, analytical description in phenomenology is interpretative in character. The business of hermeneutical phenomenology is interpreting the meaning of Being through the analysis of the various structures of Dasein. Thus, phenomenology as hermeneutic, works as the analytic of the existentiality of the existence that Dasein possesses.

Heidegger's philosophical journey consists of two phases. The earlier phase comprises the fundamental ontology aimed at clarifying the meaning of Being in general (*Sinn Von Sein*). It is an attempt at the disclosure of the ontological meaning of Dasein, the privileged entity that has priority over other entities on account of its pre-understanding of Being. It involves an interpretation of the relation of Dasein to Being from the perspective of Dasein itself. Here, Heidegger keeps himself closer to the way-side of the entity of Dasein and attempts to look towards Being which is on the other side. He considers the Being of entities through the clarification of the meaning of the Being of Dasein with temporality as its ontological meaning. Since Dasein is an entity which is to-be-in-the-world, the disclosure of the meaning of its Being discloses all other entities with-in-the-world in their Being. Thus the earlier phase of Heidegger's thought, when viewed in terms of the relation between Being and entities, points not only to the belonging-togetherness of Being and Dasein but also to the Being of other entities. Heidegger has devoted his most celebrated work *Being and Time* (*Sein Und Ziet*) to the exposition of the first stage of his philosophical enterprise. But his project of looking into the meaning of Being in general never got fully accomplished at this stage. Heidegger therefore felt the need for taking a different approach to the question of the meaning of Being, which resulted in a 'turn' (*Kehre*) in his way of thinking.

The later phase of Heidegger's thinking is centred round the 'difference' between Being and entities. Here he directs his thinking to the perdurance (*Austrag*) between Being and entities. He moves from the wayside of Dasein to the mid-way between Being and Dasein. Instead of considering Being and entities as two mutually exclusive realities, Heidegger relates them by thinking of the very difference between them. Unlike Plato who divided Being and entities into two ontologically separate realms of reality, Heidegger emphasizes the belonging togetherness of Being and entities but without nullifying the 'difference' between them. As against Plato's two-tier conception of reality, Heidegger maintains a relation of perdurance between Being and entities through his conception of concealing and revealing. That is, the concealed Being gets revealed in the being of entities through Dasein's way of Being.

Thus, in the second phase of his thinking, it is through the process of unconcealment that Heidegger reveals both the difference and togetherness of Being and entities. In this changed perspective, Heidegger's thinking of Being is based on Dasein's receptive opening to the presencing of Being. Here man's relation to Being is not one of transcendence towards Being. The relation is not one of projective understanding of Being but a receptive listening to Being. Owing to his primordial belongingness to Being, man can stand open and listen to Being. He can let himself into the primordial letting by Being. He can receive the epochal giving by Being. The authentic thinking of Being consists in man's receptive listening to the epochal calling by Being.

Heidegger's two phases of the thinking of Being may be summed up as follows: the first phase covers the area wherein Dasein in its projective transcendence and horizontal temporalizing, lays bare the meaning of its Being and that of the Being of entities with-in-the-world. The second phase encompasses the realm wherein Being gives itself epochally in the mode of time to the waiting mortals. While his principal work *Being and Time* comprises the first phase of Heidegger's thought, the works other than *Being and Time* embody the second phase of his thought.

Just as Heidegger's philosophical enterprise consists of two phases, his *Being and Time* is originally designed to have two parts, besides Introduction. Two parts are aimed at accomplishing two distinct tasks. Part One is devoted to the task of the interpretation of Dasein in terms of temporality, and the explication of time as the transcendental horizon for the question of Being. And Part Two is aimed at the task of dealing with the basic features of a phenomenological 'destruction' of the history of ontology, with the problematic of temporality as the clue. Each part has been divided into three divisions. The three divisions of Part One are as follows: (1) The Preparatory Fundamental Analysis of Dasein, (2) Dasein and Temporality, and (3) Time and Being. And the three divisions of Part two are: (1) Kant's Doctrine of Schematism and Time as a Preliminary Stage in a Problematic of Temporality, (2) the Ontological Foundation of Descartes' *cogito sum*, and how the Medieval Ontology has been taken over into the Problematic of the *res cogitans*, and (3) Aristotle's Essay on Time as Providing a way of Discriminating the Phenomenal Basis and the Limits of Ancient Ontology. But the important fact to note is that Part Two and the third division of Part One have never appeared. Since there happened to be a 'turn' in Heidegger's thinking, he did not attempt at completing them. Instead, he devoted his time and thought to the writing of other works. Thus, the text of *Being and Time* comprises the discussion of the first two divisions of Part One only. However, Heidegger has successfully presented a clear and comprehensive perspective of Dasein in *Being and Time* even in its unfinished form. *Being and Time* remains to be the most celebrated work in the filed of phenomenology, despite its incompletion. Undoubtedly, the treatise is a massive analysis of human reality, the *sine qua non* for understanding the meaning of Being.

C. Scope of the Study

This study proposes to deal only with the first phase of Heidegger's thought. Its scope is limited to the interpretation of the Being of Dasein as it is enshrined by Heidegger in his *Being and Time*. It confines itself to the exposition of Heidegger's conception of Dasein through which the meaning of Being is revealed. The study does not venture on Heidegger's later phase of thought which he has expounded in his later works that followed *Being and Time*. The motivating factor that has prompted me to undertake this study is to make a thorough investigation into one of the very important philosophical conceptions, namely, the conception of Dasein, as it has been dealt with by an equally important thinker like Heidegger. Concept of man is central not only to Heidegger's thought but to philosophical thinking as a whole. The main objective of the study is to present a clear and detailed perspective of Dasein by being faithful to the original text of *Being and Time*.

The entire discussion in the book is embedded in six chapters. Chapter one is "Introduction." It presents, in brief, the life and philosophy of Heidegger. It also highlights the objective and the scope of the study. Chapter Two viz., "Dasein and the Question of the Meaning of Being," discusses the formal structure, the ontic and ontological priority of the question of Being. It discusses Dasein's three-fold priority to the question of Being and the task of destroying the history of ontology. It includes an ontological analytic of Dasein, besides a detailed description of the phenomenological method of investigation. Chapter III, namely, "Dasein and Being-in-the-World," comprises an exposition of Being-in-the-world as the fundamental mode of Dasein. It discusses in detail the three constituent items of Being-in-the-world, namely, the worldhood of the world, the entity which has Being-in-the-world as a way of its Being, and Being-in as such. Chapter IV, viz., "Dasein, Care and Death," explicates care as the basic existential phenomenon of Dasein's Being and it interprets truth as the disclosedness of the Dasein's Being. It deals with the phenomenon of death as Dasein's ownmost possibility into which Dasein has been thrown and which it can never outstrip. The existential-ontological conception of Dasein's authentic Being-towards-death also has been elaborated. Chapter V, namely, "Dasein, Authenticity and Temporality," deals with authenticity as Dasein's potentiality-for-Being, and temporality as the primordial basis of Dasein's existentiality. In it, conscience and resoluteness have been explained as the call of care. Dasein's Being as a whole is exhibited as being finite by interpreting all its structures in terms of temporality. With this the phenomenological investigation into the nature and structure of Dasein as a whole comes to an end. And thus the task of answering the question of the meaning of Being in its totality gets accomplished. Chapter VI is "Conclusion." Besides summing up the whole discussion, it comprises a critical appraisal of Heidegger's thought as contained in his *Being and Time.*

Chapter II

Dasein and the Question of the Meaning of Being

Martin Heidegger begins his magnum opus, *Being and Time* by deploring that the question of the meaning of Being[1] has been forgotten. The present-day metaphysics has failed to give serious attention to the question of the meaning of Being which inspired even the classical philosophers like Plato and Aristotle who dealt with it with utmost care and effort. The question no doubt has persisted in its various dimensions from ancient times down to the logic of Hegel. But what has so far been unravelled about it is only fragmentary and incipient. The question which has long been trivialized should now be taken "as a theme for actual investigation,"[2] says Heidegger. He holds that a dogma has been developed about the question of the meaning of Being since the Greek's initial contribution towards its interpretation. The dogma is that the question is superfluous and worthy of complete neglect. The dogma is that Being is the emptiest of all concepts and resists all attempts at definition. But Heidegger contends that the concept of Being as such does not require any definition. We use the term "Being" so commonly and constantly that we have an immediate understanding of it. Being which was something obscure and hidden to ancient philosophers should be made clear and self-evident by the modern thinkers.

A. Presuppositions about the Question of the Meaning of Being

According to Heidegger, in ancient ontology there are three presuppositions about Being. The first one is that Being is the most universal concept. The second is that the concept of Being is indefinable. And the third is that Being is the most self-evident of all concepts (*BT* 22-23). Heidegger holds that the universality of Being is not that of a class or genus but the transcendence of it. Merely to say that Being is the most universal concept is to say that Being is the darkest and enigmatic of all concepts. Universality does not imply that Being is a clear and distinct concept which does not require any more understanding and interpretation. Heidegger holds that the second presupposition that Being is an indefinable concept rightly follows from the first one. Indefinability of Being means that Being cannot be conceived as an entity. It can neither be derived from higher concepts nor can it be presented through the lower ones. Indefinability does not imply that the question of the meaning of Being cannot become 'a problematic.' It only means that we cannot apply to Being the concept of definition which we find in traditional logic. It does not eliminate the primordial importance of the question of meaning of Being but "demands that we look that question in the face" (*BT* 23). And the third presupposition that Being is self-evident gives an impression that Being is accessible to "an average kind of intelligibility" (*BT* 23) which, according to Heidegger, implies that Being is unintelligible. He contends that these presuppositions about Being have fostered the belief that an inquiry into the question of Being is impossible and unnecessary.

Heidegger is of the view that Being is very much prevalent in our daily parlance and living. Whenever we cognize anything or make an assertion about it we make use of 'Being.' We experience a semblance of 'Being' in comporting ourselves towards entities or towards ourselves. We use the expression "Being" in several other ways; we hold it to be intelligible without much difficulty, we treat it as easily understandable as the statements like "I am happy" or "The sky is blue." But Heidegger maintains that this kind of understanding of Being is a priori enigmatic. The so-called evidence or the supposition that we already have a comprehension of Being does not guarantee that Being is fully manifested. It does not absolve us of raising the question of the meaning of Being. Heidegger says, "The very fact that we already live in an understanding of Being and that the meaning of Being is still veiled in darkness proves that it is necessary in principle to raise this question again" (*BT* 23).

Heidegger treats the three presuppositions mentioned above as there prejudices. The prejudices have been a barrier to discover a proper answer to the question of the meaning of Being. They have rendered the question itself "obscure and without direction" (*BT* 24). Heidegger therefore holds that there is an urgent need to revive the question of the meaning of Being. We have to work out an adequate way of formulating this fundamental question.

B. The Formal Structure of the Question of Being

Heidegger maintains that the question of the meaning of Being is the most fundamental one which must be clearly *formulated.* The question must be made transparent in a proper way. It must be explained from the standpoint which can render it as a very special one. It must be unravelled in its own distinctive character. Heidegger writes, "The question of the meaning of Being must be *formulated.* If it is a—or even *the*—fundamental question, such questioning needs the suitable perspicuity."[2] He holds that every inquiry is a seeking (*Suchen*) which is guided beforehand by what is sought. An inquiry is a cognizant seeking for an entity with regard to its fact that it is and with regard to its Being as it is. As a cognizant seeking an inquiry can take the form of investigation (*Untersuchen*). Investigation is laying bare that which the question is asked about. It is ascertaining the character of that which is in question by probing into it.

Any inquiry is always an inquiry about something. It always has as its object *that which is asked about (sein ge fragtes)*. Besides what is asked about, an inquiry also has *that which is interrogated* (*ein begfragtes*). Furthermore, in what is asked about there lies also *that which is to be found out by the asking* (*das erfragte*). Heidegger says that an inquiry reaches its goal by determining and conceptualizing that which is asked about by discovering that which is interrogated and that which is to be found. This is what is really intended by the inquiry which is a cognizant seeking and investigation. Heidegger holds that an inquiry is nothing but the behaviour of the questioner. An inquiry therefore is always of an entity having its own character of Being. So an inquiry may either be casual or serious. It is in a serious type of inquiry that we can explicitly formulate the question about anything. The serious inquiry becomes transparent to itself only when all constituent factors of the question have themselves become transparent. Inquiry must always be guided before hand by what is sought. The inquiry about Being must be guided by Being only, for it is Being that is being sought. That is, the meaning of Being must already be available to us. In fact, we always conduct our activities in such a way that we have an understanding of Being. It is out of this understanding that there arises the explicit question of the meaning of Being. It is this understanding that also leads us to the conception of Being. We do not *know* what is Being. Yet, in asking the question 'What is Being'? We keep the 'is' within our understanding. The verb 'is' is a testimony to our vague and average understanding of Being. At this stage, we may not be able to fix conceptually what the 'is' signifies. We may not know the horizon in terms of which we can grasp the meaning of Being. The understanding of Being is dim and fluctuating. It borders on mere acquaintance with the word "is." Nevertheless, the very indefiniteness of Being at this level is still a fact and a positive phenomenon which needs to be clarified (*BW* 46).

An investigation of the meaning of Being cannot be clear at the very outset. If we are to obtain the clue required for interpreting the average understanding of Being, we must develop the concept of Being. It is in the light of this concept and the ways in which it may be explicitly understood that we can make out the meaning of the obscured, unillumined understanding of Being. We can grasp the possible and even inevitable hindrances to an explicit illumination of the meaning of Being. Thus the inquiry into the question of Being is not something entirely new and unfamiliar. We begin the inquiry with the vague and average understanding of Being contained in the traditional theories about it. Devoid of ancient opinions about Being, we cannot grasp the meaning of Being at all even proximally.

According to Heidegger there are three constitutive factors of inquiry into the meaning of Being. The first one is *that which is asked about*. What is it that which is asked about? It is Being that which is asked about. Being determines entities as entities. It is on the basis of this Being that entities are already understood. This Being of entities 'is' not itself an entity. Being is essentially different from the entities. So it has to be discovered in an essentially different way. Being has to be exhibited in a unique way of its own. Its meaning has to be conceived in the way which is in contrast with the way in which the meaning of the entities is determined. Heidegger says, "As what is asked about, Being thus requires its own kind of demonstration which is essentially different from the discovery of being. Hence what is to be *ascertained*, the meaning of Being will require its own conceptualization, which again is essentially distinct from the concepts in which beings receive their determination of meaning" (*BW* 47).

The second factor of the inquiry into the meaning of Being is that which is interrogated. What is that which is interrogated? Heidegger says that entities (*seiendes*)[3] themselves are that which is interrogated. Only entities are interrogated because Being is the Being of entities and also because Being constitutes what is asked about. Entities are questioned as regards their Being. They become accessible as they are in themselves only when the characteristics of their Being are ascertained without falsification. So the inquiry demands that we obtain in advance the right way of access to entities. There are many things which we designate as 'being' (*seiend*). We designate them as 'being' in several ways. Everything is 'being.' We encounter 'being' in everything we have in view, in everything we talk about and comport ourselves in any way. Being is also revealed in what we are and how we are. Heidegger declares, "Being lies in fact that something is, and in its Being as it is; in reality; in presence-at-hand; in subsistence; in validity; in Dasein; in the 'there is'" (*BT* 26).

The third factor that constitutes the question about the meaning of Being is the 'entity' that raises the question about the meaning of Being. What is the entity that asks the question about the meaning of Being? Heidegger holds that of all the entities it is Dasein[4] that asks the question about the meaning of Being. Dasein is the right entity which alone can have a genuine access to Being. Dasein alone is capable of the activities like looking, understanding and conceiving something; it alone has the capacity of choosing and having access to something. Heidegger says that all these ways of behaving constitute the ways of inquiry into the meaning of Being. They are also the modes of Being for Dasein. So Dasein has the privilege of being the inquirer into Being; it has the priority over all other beings in having access to Being. Dasein should be the point of departure for the disclosure of Being. The question of Being can be explicitly formulated and made completely transparent only by making Dasein as the starting point of our inquiry. It is only in the entity of Dasein that the meaning of Being is clearly understood and discerned. It is only by choosing the entity of Dasein as the inquirer that Being can properly be looked at, and conceptually grasped and elucidated. It is only by making the inquirer transparent in his Being that the question of Being can be worked out adequately. For, the very asking of the question about the Being constitutes Dasein's mode of Being. Dasein derives its essential character of being an inquirer from what is inquired about, namely, Being. Heidegger asserts that Dasein is none other than ourselves. We the inquirers are Dasein. Dasein is the entity which each one of us is. Inquiry is one of the possibilities of Dasein's Being. Therefore in order to formulate the question of the meaning of Being, we must first clearly explain Dasein with regard to its Being. Heidegger says, "Thus to work out the question of Being means to make a being—he who questions—perspicuous in his Being. Asking this question, as a mode of *being* of a being, is itself essentially determined by what is asked about in it—Being. This being which we ourselves in each case are and which includes inquiry among the possibilities of its Being we formulate terminologically as Dasein. The explicit and lucid formulation of the question of the meaning of Being requires a prior suitable explication of a being (Dasein) with regard to its "Being" (*BW* 48).

C. The Ontological Priority of Question of Being

According to Heidegger the question of Being is a peculiar one; we have to examine a series of its fundamental considerations in order to work it out and solve it. We have to delimit the question adequately with regard to its function, aim and motives. Only then its distinctive features will be brought fully to light. Although the question has venerable origins, it lacks a satisfactory formulation and definite answer. The purpose of the question is not a matter of soaring and free-floating speculation about the most general of generalities. On the contrary, of all the questions, the question about Being is "both the most basic and the most concrete" (*BW* 29).

To Heidegger, ontology is the right 'science' for the study of the meaning of Being. Of all the disciplines—mathematics, physics, biology, theology and humanities—ontology alone constitutes the proper study of the question of Being. Ontological (*Ontologisch*) inquiry is more primordial than the ontical (*ontisch*)[5] inquiry of the positive sciences. Ontological inquiry is concerned primarily with Being, whereas ontical inquiry is concerned primarily with entities and the facts about them. Ontological inquiry into the Being of entities should not remain to be naïve and opaque. It should progress by the discussion of the meaning of Being in general; it should construct a non-deductive genealogy of the different possible ways of Being. It must first aim at understanding the real meaning of the expression "Being." Heidegger writes, "Basically, all ontology, no matter how rich and firmly compacted a system of categories it has at its disposal, remains blind and perverted from its ownmost aim, if it has not first adequately clarified the meaning of Being and conceived this clarification as its fundamental task" (*BT* 31). Thus the proper understanding of ontological research shows that it should give priority to the question of Being. This priority is precisely the ontological priority of the question of Being. Giving ontological priority does not mean mere resumption of the venerable tradition of the question of Being; but it is rather going beyond the tradition in which the question has been opaque.

D. The Ontical Priority of the Question of Being

Besides the ontological priority which is objectively scientific, the question of Being has another priority, namely, the ontical priority. The question takes ontical priority because Dasein is ontically a distinct entity. Dasein is ontically distinguished by the fact that, in its very Being, that Being is an *issue* for it. Dasein is not an entity which simply occurs among other entities. In Dasein, Being is always in question. The question of Being is "a constitutive state of Dasein's Being" (*BT* 32). In its Being, Dasein has a relationship to Being. The relationship is such that Dasein's Being itself is one of Being. It means that Dasein has some access through which it understands itself in its Being. Being is disclosed to Dasein through its own Being. This is the peculiarity of the entity of Dasein. Heidegger says, "Understanding of Being is itself a definite characteristic of Dasein's Being. Dasein is ontically distinctive in that it is ontological" (*BT* 32).

E. Dasein's Three-fold Priority to the Question of Being

Heidegger says that Dasein has a threefold priority over all other entities to the question of the meaning of Being. Firstly, Dasein has an ontical priority over other entities, since its essence lies in the fact that in each case it has its Being to be and has it as its own. This character of having-to-be (*zusein*) its Being as its own, endows Dasein with two other characteristics, namely, existence (*existinz*) and mineness (*jumeingkeit*). Existence is the kind of Being towards which Dasein can somehow and always comport itself in one way or another. The essence of Dasein can be conceived only in terms of its Being which is designated as existence. That is, the essence of Dasein lies in its existence and it understands itself in terms of existence only. In other wards, Dasein understands itself only in terms of the possibilities of itself. The possibilities are such that in them Dasein can either be of itself or not be of itself. They may be either given, chosen or in which Dasein has grown up already. Heidegger says, "Existence is decided only by each Dasein itself in the manner of seizing upon or neglecting such possibilities. We came to terms with the question of existence always only through existence itself" (*BW* 55).

Heidegger argues that Dasein's existence is not the same as the traditional concept of existence. In tradition, the concept of existence has been used indiscriminately. The term "existence" is applied in almost the same sense to everything—God, man, animal and stone. But the existence of Dasein is distinctive in that it speaks of Dasein's ability to understand Being. Existence speaks of the special relation Dasein has to its potentiality for Being which can be said only of Dasein. Dasein's is entirely different from the existence of other entities or beings, "Rocks are but they do not exist; trees are, but they do not exist; God is, but he does not exist. Dasein alone exists."[6]

The other special characteristic of Dasein, namely, mineness is closely related to "existence." As it has already been mentioned, Dasein is primarily existence in the mode of having-to-be. So it has to choose constantly from the possible ways for it to be. Dasein is never a finished or self-inclosed product. It can never remain without having to choose from its possibilities. Dasein is its own possibilities. It does not have them as a property (*eigenschaft*). That is, the Being which is an issue for Dasein in its very Being and in each case is its very Being. This precisely is the mineness of Dasein's Being. "Dasein is in each case mine-to-be in one way or another."[7]

The second priority that Dasein has to Being over all other entities is ontological in character. Dasein's ontological priority follows from its ontical priority elucidated above. In being ontically distinctive, Dasein is rendered ontological. That is, Dasein's ontical character of understanding Being endows Dasein with an ontological characteristic of interpreting Being. Since Dasein determines itself on the background of its own existence, Dasein is in itself ontological in character. It possesses an understanding of the Being of itself as well as the Being of all other beings which are unlike itself. It understands Being in general in a manner constitutive of the understanding of its existence. But Heidegger says that the fact of Dasein's ontological priority signifies that Dasein, at this stage, has only a pre-ontological understanding of Being. Dasein's "Being-ontological" does not tantamount to developing an ontology which is a theoretical inquiry explicitly devoted to the meaning of Being of all entities including Dasein. Besides the ontical and ontological priority, Dasein can be said to have a third priority, namely, the ontico-ontological priority. Dasein has this priority, since it possesses an understanding of the Being of all entities which are different from it and have a character other than its own. Dasein possesses this kind of understanding, besides possessing an understanding of Being in relation to its own being which is of the nature of existence and mineness. Heidegger writes, "Dasein accordingly takes priority in several ways over all other beings. The first priority is an ontic one: this being is defined in its Being by existence. The second priority is an ontological one: on the basis of its determination as existence Dasein is in itself ontological. But just as originally Dasein possesses—in a manner constitutive of its understanding of existence—an understanding of the Being of all beings unlike itself. Dasein therefore has its third priority as the ontic-ontological condition of the possibility of all ontologies" (*BW* 56).

With the three-fold priority to the question of Being Dasein turns out to be the primary entity which must be interrogated. Dasein is the only right entity which must be questioned and analyzed ontologically. Dasein is the privileged entity which must be worked out in an ontologically adequate manner. Only then does the inquiry into the question of the meaning of Being become plain and transparent. Heidegger says, "If to Interpret the meaning of Being becomes our task, Dasein is not only the primary entity to be interrogated; it is also that entity which already comports itself, in its Being, towards what we are asking about when we ask this question. But in that case the question of Being is nothing other than the radicalization of an essential tendency-of-Being which belongs to Dasein itself—the pre-ontological understanding Being" (*BW* 35).

Thus the threefold priority of Dasein over other beings to the question of the meaning of Being makes fundamental ontology possible. Fundamental ontology is an inquiry into the meaning of Being in general. Fundamental ontology is not just one of the various ontical sciences but a primordial science which makes all of them possible. That is, the ontical sciences of entities, otherwise known as positive sciences, arise out of the fundamental ontology which is the ontological science of Being. Heidegger regards fundamental ontology itself as philosophy proper. He says that philosophy as fundamental ontology must be sought in the existential analytic of Dasein. He also holds that it is from the fundamental ontology alone that all other ontologies can take their origin (*BW* 34).

The analytic of Dasein is that in which Dasein always understands itself in terms of its existence. Only a particular Dasein decides its existence, either by taking hold or by neglecting it. Existence thus is the determining character of Dasein. Dasein gets its existence straightened out only through existence itself. The question of existence is one of Dasein's ontical affairs. And the understanding of Dasein in terms of the ontical is called "existentielle."[8] The question of existence does not require that its ontological structure should be theoretically transparent. The ontological structure of existence aims at the analysis (*auseinanderlegung*) of what constitutes existence. The context (*zusammenhang*) of such structure is called *existentiality*. Existentiality is the state of Being that is constitutive of the entities that exist. And the analytic of the ontological structure of existence is called *existential*. The ontological analytic of Dasein always requires that existentiality is considered before hand. The idea of existentiality already includes the idea of Being. So the analytic of Dasein "depends on working out beforehand the question about the meaning of Being in general" (*BT* 33), avers Heidegger.

F. The Ontological Analytic of Dasein

Dasein is the primary entity for formulating the question of Being. It is the primordial object of interrogation for the task of understanding the meaning of Being. Dasein takes over the principal role within the question of Being, for Dasein is immediately accessible to us. Ontically Dasein is not only close but closest to us. We are it. Each of us is the Dasein; we ourselves are the Dasein (*BT* 36). Heidegger thus arrives at the privileged ontic pole in the being of Dasein. It is from this pole that he launches an ontological inquiry into the question of Being. The inquiry involves the two-fold task: one positive, and the other negative. The former consists in the ontological analysis of Dasein in view of elucidating the meaning of Being in general, and later, in the destruction of the history of ontology.[9]

In designating the task of formulating the question of Being, it is Dasein as an entity which serves as the primary object of interrogation. Since Dasein is ontico-ontologically prior to other entities and since it is immediately accessible to us, Dasein has to be understood and interpreted proximally. Heidegger at the same time says that although Dasein is ontically closest to us, ontologically it is farthest to us. But Dasein's ownmost Being is such that it has an understanding of that Being. Dasein already maintains itself in each case as if its Being has been interpreted in some manner. But this pre-ontological interpretation of Dasein's Being by itself cannot be taken as an appropriate clue. This way of understanding of Being cannot be said to emerge when Dasein's ownmost state of Being is considered as an ontological theme. The Being of Dasein has a tendency of understanding its own Being in terms of the world. The world is the entity towards which Dasein comports itself proximally and in a way which is essentially constant. In Dasein and in its own understanding of Being lies not only the understanding of the world but also the way the world is understood. The understanding of the world is reflected back ontologically upon the way in which Dasein itself gets interpreted. Heidegger says, "Thus because Dasein is ontico-ontologically prior, its own specific state of Being (if we understand this in the sense of Dasein's 'categorical structure') remains concealed from it. Dasein is ontically 'closest' to itself and ontologically farthest; but pre-ontologically it is surely not a stranger" (*BT* 37).

Heidegger thus points out that the understanding of Being belongs to Dasein. The understanding of Being develops or decays with whatever kind of Being Dasein may possess at the time. Accordingly there are many ways in which Dasein has been interpreted. All these interpretations are at Dasein's disposal. That is, Dasein's capacities, powers, possibilities and vicissitudes have been studied by various disciplines like philosophical psychology, anthropology, ethics, poetry, history, biography and so on. Each discipline has studied Dasein's ways of behaviour in its own different fashion. But Heidegger contends that their studies of Dasein hardly deal with its primordial existentiality. They deal more with the existentiell primordiality of Dasein. Primordial existentiality and existentiell primordiality may not be necessarily related. Yet they are not mutually exclusive. Existentiell interpretation of Dasein demands an existential analytic of Dasein. So the basic structures of Dasein have to be adequately worked out. They have to be studied with an explicit orientation towards the problem of Being itself. Only then will the results hitherto gained in interpreting Dasein get their existential justification (*BT* 37).

Heidegger therefore maintains that the analytic of Dasein is of fundamental importance in the explication of the question of Being. So also obtaining the access leading to Dasein is equally important. Dogmatic interpretations of Dasein also have to be avoided. We cannot apply just any idea of Being to Dasein, however self-evident that idea may be. We cannot force any of the 'categories' upon Dasein. On the contrary, we have to choose such a way of access to Dasein that can show Dasein as it is *proximally* and for the most part, in its everdayness. We have to choose such a kind of interpretation that Dasein can show itself in itself and from itself (*an ihm selbst von ihm selbst her*). That is, we have to explicate the structures of Dasein in its everydayness. These structures should not be accidental but essential ones, which the factical Dasein possesses in every kind of its Being. Dasein should exhibit these structures as determining the character of its Being: "Thus by having regard for the basic state of everydayness," says Heidegger, "we shall bring out the Being of this entity (Dasein) in a preparatory fashion" (*BT* 38).

It is only by taking Dasein in its everydayness that the analytic of Dasein remains wholly oriented towards working out the meaning of Being. The analytic has to be strictly confined to Dasein's everydayness. The analytic is only provisional. It does not provide a complete ontology of Dasein. Nevertheless, the analytic is not an incomplete one. It brings out the Being of Dasein without interpreting its meaning. It is only a preparatory procedure to lay bare the horizon for interpreting the Being, in the most primordial manner. However, the analytic will be repeated on a higher level when once it arrives at the horizon for interpreting Being. It will be revisited on "an authentically ontological basis" (*BT* 38), for a complete ontology of Dasein. In the absence of a complete ontology of Dasein a philosophical anthropology cannot have a philosophically adequate basis.

Heidegger says that Dasein is an entity which, in its Being, comports itself towards its Being. As an entity with the Being which comports itself towards itself, Dasein is delivered over to its own Being. So Dasein is the only entity for which Being is an issue to itself. The essence (*Wesen*) of Dasein lies in its 'to be' (*Zu-sein*). In other words, the Being-what-it-is (*Was-sein*) can be conceived only in terms of its existence (*existenz*). The term "existence "comes from the Germen "exsisteren" which means "to stand out" or "to examine itself." Unlike other entities, Dasein is the entity, which alone can stand out of itself and examine itself. That is why Heidegger chooses to designate the Being of Dasein as existence. In this sense, Dasein is entirely different from the entities that are present-at-hand. Dasein is not a table, a chair, or a pen which is present-at-hand. The characteristics which Dasein exhibits are not like the "properties" of an entity which is present-at-hand. The characteristics are not properties (*eigen-*

schaftlich) present-at-hand but the possible ways for Dasein to be. All the characteristics which Dasein possesses are of its Being only. They stand not for its "what" (as if it were a table, house or tree) but for its Being only. Besides existence which is the essence of Dasein, mineness is another aspect of its essence. The Being of Dasein is *in each case mine*. So Dasein is not an instance of things that are present-at-hand and whose Being is a matter of indifference to them. Since Dasein has in each case mineness (*Jemeinigkeit*), its Being is never a matter of indifference to it. Unlike in the case of entities such as things, it is necessary to use personal pronouns like "I am," "You are," "He is" when one addresses the entity of Dasein. In each case Dasein is mine to be in one way or another. It has always made some sort of decision as to the way in which it is in each case mine. In each case, Dasein is essentially its own possibility. So it can, in its very Being, "choose" itself and win itself; it can also lose itself and never win itself; it can also seem to either lose or win itself. In doing so, Dasein exhibits two modes of Being, namely, authenticity and inanthenticity. These modes are grounded in the fact that Dasein is characterized by mineness (*BT* 68).

As an entity which is characterized by existence and mineness, Dasein is a being of self-determination. It determines itself in the light of a possibility which it is itself and which it somehow understands. Heidegger calls it the formal meaning of Dasein's existential constitution. So the ontological interpretation of Dasein is possible only by developing (the problematic of) its Being from the existentiality of its existence. The interpretation should not construe Dasein in terms of some concrete possible idea of existence. It should not be interpreted with the differentiated character of some definite way of existing. But Dasein should be uncovered (*aufgedecckt*) in the undifferentiated character which it has proximally and for the most part. Heidegger calls this undifferentiated character of Dasein its everydayness or averageness (*Durchschnittlichkeit*). This everydayness "is not nothing, but a positive phenomenal characteristic of Dasein" (*BT* 69).

The average everydayness is ontically proximate for Dasein; it is the closest and well known to it. So also it is ontologically farthest and not known at all. It is often forgotten and its ontological signification is overlooked in explicating Dasein. Average everydayness is not a mere aspect of Dasein. It is one of the important apriori structures of its existentiality. In it Dasein's Being is an issue for it in a definite way. It is in the mode of average everydayness that Dasein comports itself towards itself. The explication of Dasein in its average everydayness does not give its average structures that are hazy and indefinite. It gives the pregnant structures that are indistinguishable from certain ontological characteristics of an authentic Being of Dasein.

The analytic of Dasein is the explication of the structures of Dasein's existence in its average everydayness. In it, Dasein's characteristics of Being are defined in terms of existentiality. Heidegger calls these characteristics *existentialia.* He sharply distinguishes them from what we call *categories.* The categories are the characteristics of Being for entities, whereas existentialia are the characteristics of Being for Dasein. Categories and existentialia correspond to two different kinds of entities. The former correspond to an entity which is addressed by the pronoun "what," while the latter correspond to an entity which is addressed by the pronoun "who." The character of the Being of the former is presence-at-hand whereas that of the latter is existence. The connection between these two modes of characters of Being can be analyzed only by clarifying the horizon for the question of Being (*BT* 71).

Heidegger distinguishes the analytic of Dasein from Psychology, Anthropology and Biology. The former precedes the latter three, in so far as the ontological question is concerned. The analytic of Dasein differs from philosophical anthropology which posits the 'I' or the Subject as the Soul-substance. Philosophical anthropology starting from Descartes treats the "I" as the person endowed with 'thing hood.' It also uses the terms "soul," "spirit," "consciousness" and so on to refer to the "subject." It uses them to refer to entities with some definite phenomenal domains which do not refer to the question of Being. Philosophical Anthropology has failed to inquire into the Being of the entities designated by spirit, consciousness or soul. The question of the Being of Dasein has a dimension which Physical Anthropology of person fails to enter. The analytic of Dasein also differs from the Christian Anthropology which defines man as a rational animal endowed with reason. The traditional Anthropology understands the Being of man only in the sense of occurring and being-present-at-hand. Even the idea of 'transcendence'—that man is something that reaches beyond himself—which is rooted in the Christian Anthropology can hardly be said to have touched upon the question of Being. Whereas the analytic of Dasein regards the person as a performer of intentional acts which are bound together by the unity of meaning. It does not objectify the human acts and depersonalize the person. It does not reduce the personal Being to psychical Being by taking acts as psychological objects. The analytic treats acts as those that are performed by the person who is a performer. Acts are experienced in their performance and given in reflection. So acts are intentional and the person is essentially the performer of intentional acts with a unity of meaning. Heidegger therefore contends that the analytic of Dasein differs from Psychology and Biology also. Both Psychology and Biology exhibit unmistakable anthropological tendencies. They cannot raise and answer the question of the meaning of Being that belongs to Dasein. They fail to fathom the ontological foundations for the interpretation of the Being of Dasein. Heidegger writes, "In suggesting that Anthropology, Psychology and Biology all fail to give an unequivocal and ontologically adequate answer to the question about the *kind of Being* which belongs to those entities which we ourselves are, we are not passing judgments on the positive work of these disciplines. We must always bear in mind, however, that these ontological foundations can never be disclosed by subsequent hypotheses derived from empirical material, but they are always 'there' already, even when that empirical material simply gets *collected*. If positive research fails to see these foundations and holds them to be self-evident, this by no means proves that they are not basic or that they are not problematic in a more radical sense than any thesis of positive sciences can ever be (*BT* 75).

G. The Analytic of Dasein and Temporality

Heidegger holds that having shown Dasein in its everydayness, the analytic has to demonstrate temporality as the meaning of Dasein's Being. The demonstration involves interpretation of the essential structures of the factical Dasein as the modes of temporality. Interpretation of Dasein as temporality prepares the ground for obtaining an answer to the question of the meaning of Being. As it has already been mentioned, Dasein possesses pre-ontological Being as its ontically constitutive state. Dasein is an entity which alone understands and interprets something like Being. And it always interprets Being with *time* as its standpoint. Heidegger therefore holds that time must be brought to light by genuinely conceiving it as the horizon for all understanding and interpretation of Being. He says, "In order for us to discern this, *time* needs to be explicated primordially as the horizon for the understanding of Being, and in terms of temporality as the Being of Dasein, which understands Being" (*BT* 39).

Heidegger's conception of time as the horizon for understanding and interpretation of Being is distinct from the time as understood in its ordinary sense. The ordinary way of understanding and conceiving time is prevalent in the traditional interpretations of it. It has persisted from Aristotle to Bergson and even later. Heidegger maintains that both the traditional concept of time and the ordinary way of understanding time in general have sprung from the notion of temporality only. The task of the analytic is to show how they have come about. The analytic thereby has to restore autonomy to the ordinary conception of time. It has to distinguish it from Bergson's thesis that the psychological time, the time that one has in mind is nothing but space. Heidegger is of the view that time has for long functioned as an ontological and ontical criterion for discriminating the various realms of entities. It is on the background of time that a distinction has been made between temporal entities like natural processes and historical happenings, and non-temporal entities like spatial and numerical relationships. A contrast has been made between the propositions of timeless significance and the propositions of temporal meaning. There has been a cleavage between temporal entities and supra-temporal eternality. Efforts have also been made to bridge the cleavage between them. But Heidegger contends that the discrimination, the contrast and the cleavage as well as the attempts at bridging the cleavage are naïve, since the term "temporal" is used simply in the sense of being (*seined*) 'in time.' The meaning of time in traditional and ordinary understanding is obscure and enigmatic. Heidegger admits that time has a distinctive ontological function. It really works as a criterion for distinguishing between various realms of Being. Time has acquired this self-evident ontological function of its own accord. But there is a need to investigate how 'time' has acquired this distinctive and self-evident ontological function. We have to unravel and discover how time has gained the authentic ontological significance of being the criterion for distinguishing between various realms of entities and their Being. It is necessary to find out how time has maintained itself its status of being ontologically relevant to this day. Heidegger therefore says that the treatment of the question of the meaning of Being should enable us to show that "the central problematic of all ontology is rooted in the phenomenon of time, if rightly seen and rightly explained" (*BT* 40).

He maintains that Being can be grasped only by taking time into consideration. Being has to be conceived in terms of time. It must be made visible in its temporal character. Only then the various modes and derivations of Being can become intelligible. In this sense the term "temporal" does not mean simply 'being in time.' Even the 'non-temporal' and 'supra-temporal' entities become 'temporal' with regard to their Being. They become temporal not only in the sense of being in contrast with the entities that are in time. They also become temporal in the positive sense of being in time themselves. This shows that Heidegger has given temporality a different signification. He employs the term "temporal" to signify the primordial determination of the meaning of the modes and characteristics of Being. The way in which their meaning is determined in terms of time Heidegger calls "*Temporal* determinateness" (*BT* 40). Thus the fundamental ontology of interpreting Being as such includes working out the temporality of Being.

H. The Task of Destruction[10] of the History of Ontology

Heidegger is of the view that Dasein finds its meaning in temporality. Temporality is the condition for Dasein's historicality. Historicality is a temporal kind of Being which Dasein alone possesses. It is constitutive of Dasein's determinate character. In this, historicality is not only distinct from but also prior to what is called "history." It stands for the state of Being that is constitutive of Dasein's historizing as such. It is only on the basis of historizing that even world-history is possible.

In its factical Being, Dasein *is* its past. It is 'what' it already was. Its past is as it were, pushing itself along behind it. Dasein possesses the past as a property which is still present-at-hand. Dasein 'is' its past in the way of its own Being which historicizes itself out of its future. Dasein has grown up in a traditional way of interpreting itself. It understands itself in terms of the way of being which it had in the past. It understands itself in terms of the understanding of Being it had at that time. It is by this understanding that the possibilities of Dasein's Being are disclosed and regulated. In this sense, Dasein's past, namely, the past of its 'generation' does not *follow along after* Dasein but always goes ahead of it (*BT* 41).

Heidegger says that Dasein can discover the historicality that has remained hidden. It can pay proper attention to tradition and study it explicitly. There is a way of discovering and studying tradition. There is a way of disclosing that which tradition 'transmits' and how this is transmitted. The discovery and disclosure can be performed as a task in their own right. By doing so Dasein brings itself into the kind of Being which consists in historiological inquiry and research. But histeriology is possible as a kind of Being which the inquiring Dasein may possess only because historicality is a determining characteristic for Dasein (*BW* 65).

Dasein has the latent possibility of making its own existence transparent to itself. It can inquire into the meaning of existentiality and the meaning of Being in general. By doing so, Dasein can discover its own historicality. Then the inquiry into Being itself can be characterized as historicality. In working out the question of Being, attention must be paid to the way of inquiring in which history can become histriological. By doing so, we can positively make the past our own. We can bring ourselves into full possession of the ownmost possibilities of the historiological inquiry. Heidegger therefore says that it is by first explicating Dasein in its temporality and historicality that the question of the meaning of Being must be explicated. The question of Being thus brings itself to the point where it understands itself as histeriological (*BW* 71-72).

The interpretation of the fundamental structures of Dasein will reveal that Dasein is inclined to fall back upon its world. It is also inclined to fall prey to the tradition of which it has explicitly taken hold. This tradition prevents Dasein from having its own guidance both in inquiring and choosing. The tradition forbids Dasein from having its own guidance for the understanding which is rooted in its ownmost Being. It also precludes the possibility of developing that understanding into an ontological kind of understanding. When tradition becomes an authoritative master, it blocks our access to the primordial 'sources' from which we derive concepts. It makes us oblivious of the fact that they have had such and such origin. It makes us think that there is no need of going back to these sources. Thus Dasein has had its historicality uprooted by tradition. Having lost its historicality, Dasein is without a ground of its own to stand on. Consequently, Dasein confines its interest only to the standpoints of philosophical activity alien to it. That is, Dasein seeks to forget the fact of its non-historicality by indulging itself in an exotic kind of philosophical activity. But Dasein indeed has historiological interests. It also has a zeal for interpretation which is philosophically 'objective' (*sachliche*). But it is unable to understand "the most elementary conditions which would alone enable it to go back to the past in a positive manner and make it productively its own" (*BT* 43).

As it has already been mentioned, Heidegger says that the question of the meaning of Being has not been properly attended to. The question has not been formulated adequately. It has also become quite forgotten in spite of our interest in 'metaphysics.' Greek ontology, which determines the conceptual character of philosophy even today, proves that Dasein understands itself or Being in general in terms of the 'world.' It also proves that metaphysics or ontology has arisen out of Dasein's understanding of itself. It also stands a testimony to a tradition in which Being in general is deteriorated and reduced to something self-evident. It shows that the ontology has degenerated into a kind of material which is useful only for the reworking. This is evident in the case of Hegel's philosophy which is only a restatement of the history of Being. Nevertheless, Greek ontology has travelled the path passing through the Scholastics of the Middle Ages to the transcendental philosophy of the modern times. Its essentials have also come to determine even the foundations and aims of Hegel's logic. In the course of its history, certain distinctive domains of Being have come to light. They are Descartes' *cogito*, Kant's transcendental subject, self or "I" and Hegel's reason, spirit or person. These entities have served as the primary guide for subsequent problematics. But they have not been interrogated in a way that reveals the structure of their Being. They have not been questioned so thoroughly as to reveal the meaning of Being. Heidegger contends that the history of the meaning of Being should be made transparent. To accomplish it, the hardened traditional history must be loosened up. The concealments the tradition has brought about must be dissolved. That is, we have "to destroy the traditional content of ancient ontology until we arrive at those primordial experiences in which we achieved our first ways of determining the nature of Being—the ways which have guided us ever since" (*BT* 44).

The destruction of history of ontology does not mean totally dispensing with the ontological tradition. It does not mean burying the past in nullity (*Nichtigkiet*). On the contrary, it involves staking out the positive possibilities of that tradition by keeping it within its limits. The aim of destruction is not negative but positive and indirect. The destruction is the criticism concerned with the way the question of Being is formulated. It begins by raising the question whether and to what extent the interpretation of Being and the phenomena of time have been brought together thematically. It also inquires into the question whether the problematic of temporality has been worked out in principle. Heidegger is of the view that Kant is the first and the only thinker who has gone towards investigating the dimension of temporality. But Kant could not reveal the central ontological functions of temporality. He could not have an insight into the problematic of temporality since he neglected the problem of Being and failed to provide an ontology of Dasein. Instead of giving a preliminary ontological analytic of the subjectivity of the Subject, Kant took over Descartes' position on the Subject dogmatically. As a result Kant's analysis of time remained traditional and ordinary. He could not bring the phenomenon of time back into the realm of subjectivity. He could not work out a transcendental determination of time. That is why "the decisive connection between *time* and *I think* was shrouded in utter darkness; it did not even become a problem" (*BT* 45), says Heidegger.

Heidegger maintains that Descartes also failed to provide an ontology of Dasein. With his axiom *cogito ergo sum*, Descartes could not determine the kind of Being which belongs to the *res cogitans*. That is, he did not have an insight into the Being of *I am* (*sum*). He neglected the question of Being altogether by supposing that the *cogito* is an absolutely certain entity. He regarded the *cogito* as a fundamental reality and applied to it medieval ontology which believed that the meaning of the Being of the *cogito* has been fixed as *ens creatum*. Descartes' dependence upon medieval scholasticism kept him from critically analyzing the traditional ontology. It failed him to question the ancient conception of Being and determine the ontological character of the *res cogitans*. The prejudice for medieval philosophy kept even his successors from taking the question of Being as a clue for "making any thematic ontological analytic of the mind" (*BT* 46).

Heidegger holds that the destruction of the history of ontology implies that the Greek ontology has to be interpreted in the light of the problematic of temporality. The process of destruction reveals the fact that the ancient way of interpreting the Being of entities is oriented towards the 'world' or 'nature' in the widest sense. Interpretation of Being as oriented towards the world means interpretation of Being in terms of 'time,' which signifies the 'presence' (*Anwesenheit*). That is, the entities in the world are understood and grasped in their Being with regard to a definite mode of time, namely, the *present*. Heidegger says that the Greek ontology must take its clues from Dasein itself for arriving at the structures of Being belonging to the entities. He defines Dasein as man's Being and "as that living thing whose Being is essentially determined by the potentiality for discourse" (*BT* 47). It is only by working out Dasein as the ontological clue that we can grasp the problem of Being in a more radical way. Then the 'dialectic,' either Platonic or Hegelian, becomes superfluous. What is required is not dialectic but "the simple awareness of something present-at-hand in its sheer presence-at-hand" (*BT* 48). This awareness carries with it the temporal structure of making something 'pure present.' The entities which show themselves in and for this awareness are understood in their most authentic sense. They are conceived in their presence and get interpreted in terms of the present. Heidegger is of the view that Parmenides had already but unwittingly taken this awareness as a guide to his interpretation of Being. The Greeks did not have an acquaintance with the fundamental ontological aspect of time. They had no insight into the possibility of the ontological function of time. So they merely took time itself as an entity among other entities and tried to grasp it in the structure of its Being. Consequently their way of understanding of Being is naively and inexplicitly oriented towards time. Nevertheless, Heidegger regards Aristotle as having presented the loftiest and purest temporal interpretation of Being. He regards Aristotle's essay on time as the first detailed interpretation of the phenomenon of time. He contends that all the subsequent accounts of time, whether of Bergson or Kant, operate within the Aristotelian conception of time.

Heidegger therefore contends that it is necessary to go through the process of destroying the ontological tradition. It is only then that the question of Being acquires its true concreteness. The destruction proves that the question of meaning of Being is not only unavoidable but requires to be reawakened and restated (*BT* 49).

I. The Phenomenological Method of Investigation

Heidegger holds that the question of the meaning of Being—the fundamental question of philosophy—must be treated *phenomenologically.* Phenomenology is devoid of technical devices; it neither subscribes to a 'standpoint' nor does it represent a 'direction.' The expression "phenomenology" only signifies a *methodological conception.* Its subject matter is not the *what* of the objects of philosophical investigations but rather the *how* of these investigations. It is rooted in the way we come to terms with the things themselves. So Heidegger formulates, phenomenology in terms of "To the things themselves" (*BT* 50). In this sense phenomenology is opposed to all free-floating constructions and accidental findings. It rejects the conceptions that are not properly demonstrated. It shuns the pseudo questions which appear to be real problems. The term "phenomenology" is composed of two components, viz., "phenomenon" and "logos" which would make it the *science of phenomenon.*

Heidegger says that the term "phenomenon" means "to show itself." It means that which shows itself in itself or that which becomes the manifest. It also means 'to bring to the light of day' or 'to put in the light.' In other words, phenomenon is that wherein something can become visible in itself. Accordingly, the phenomena are the totality of what lies in the light of day. They are the totality which the Greeks identified with entities. An entity is that which can show itself from itself in many ways depending upon the kind of access we have to it. It can also show itself from itself as something which in itself is *not.* In showing itself from itself, the phenomenon looks like something or other. This kind of showing Heidegger calls "seeming" (*Scheinen*). In this sense phenomenon is that which is 'semblant' or 'semblance.' It means, for instance, something which looks, like good but in actuality it is not so. But the phenomenon as that which shows itself out to be and as that which is only a semblance are structurally interconnected. The latter is founded on the former. However, Heidegger distinguishes "phenomenon" from "semblance." He reserves the term "phenomenon" to signify that which shows itself out to be from itself and in itself. "Phenomenon" stands for the positive and primordial signification of that which shows itself whereas "semblance" stands for the private modification of "phenomenon" (*BT* 51)·

However, the terms "phenomenon" and "semblance" have nothing to do with what we call an 'appearance' or 'mere appearance.' Appearing is not-showing-itself. What appears *does not* show itself. Anything which fails to show itself is also something which can never be semblance. Heidegger characterizes all indications, symptoms and symbols as having only the structure of appearing. Appearing is not a showing-itself in the sense of "phenomenon" but appearing is possible only by reason of a showing-itself of something. Heidegger says that the term "appearing" may be used in three senses. Firstly, appearing is an *announcing-itself* (*das Sich-melden*) through something that shows itself; secondly, appearing is that which in its showing-itself indicates something which does not show itself; and finally, appearing means the "phenomenon" as showing-itself in its genuine sense. But Heidegger refuses to equate "phenomenon" with "appearing" in all its senses. Indeed, the latter is dependent upon the former. He says that "phenomenon" as "that which shows itself" may be equated with those entities which are accessible through the empirical intuition in the Kantian sense. But the conception of phenomenon as the object of the Kantian empirical intuition is only formal. It is ordinary and not phenomenological in character. However, an insight into the meaning of the formal conception of phenomena is required for the understanding of the phenomenological conception of phenomena. Heidegger admits that an illustration of a phenomenological conception of a phenomenon is possible only within the horizon of the Kantian problematic. He regards Kant's forms of intuition, namely, space and time, as the 'phenomena' of phenomenology. It is only in the capacity of phenomena that space and time can show themselves to the perceiver. "The self-showing as such in itself (the forms of intuition) are phenomena of phenomenology. For, clearly space and time must be able to show themselves in this way. They must be able to become phenomena if Kant claims to make a valid transcendental statement when he says that space is the a priori 'wherein' of an order" (*BW* 78), avers Heidegger.

According to Heidegger, *logos* basically means 'discourse.' But in the history of philosophy, *logos* has been translated as 'reason,' 'judgment,' 'concept,' 'definition,' 'ground' or 'relationship.' Heidegger maintains that these renderings of *logos* are arbitrary. 'Discourse' is the only legitimate translation of *logos*. In this sense *logos* means "to make manifest what one is talking about in one's discourse" (*BT* 56). *Logos* lets be seen what the discourse is about; it does so either for the one who is doing the talking or for those who are talking with one another. Discourse lets us see something from the very thing which the discourse is about. As a genuine discourse, *logos* draws what is said from what the talk is about. As a discursive communication it makes what is talked about not only manifest but also accessible to the other party. Heidegger says that Aristotle has explicated this function of discourse more precisely. When discourse becomes fully concrete, it becomes a speaking, a vocal proclamation in words; it acquires the character of an utterance in which something is sighted. *Logos* has the structural form of synthesis in which it lets something be seen in its togetherness (*Beisammen*) with something—"to let something be seen as something" (*BW* 80).

Since the *logos* is a letting-something-be-seen, it can therefore be true or false. The truth of the *logos* is not the one that pertains to judgments. Truth as construed in the sense of agreement does not belong to the *logos*. On the contrary, the 'being-true' of the *logos* means taking the entities out of their hiddenness. It is letting them be *discovered* or seen as something unhidden. And 'being-false' is deceiving in the sense of covering up. The truth of the *logos* lies in the pure perception of the simplest determinate ways of Being which entities may possess. It discovers the Being in such a way that it can never cover up. In this, Heidegger is equating the 'being-true' of the *logos* with the Greek conception of truth as the sheer sensory perception of something. He holds that it is only in terms of this conception of truth that it is possible to understand 'a doctrine of ideas' as philosophical knowledge. He contends that both realism and idealism have missed the meaning of the Greek conception of truth (*BT* 57).

Having thus interpreted the terms "phenomenon" and "logos," Heidegger formulates the meaning of phenomenology as "to let that which shows itself be seen from itself in the very way in which it shows itself from itself" (*BT* 58). In this sense, phenomenology is quite different from theology, biology and sociology. These 'sciences' designate the objects of their study according to the subject-matter which they comprise at a particular time. Whereas, phenomenology does not designate the object of its research; nor does it characterize its subject-matter. It only informs us of the *how* with which the *what* gets handled and exhibited. As a science 'of' phenomena, phenomenology means grasping its objects in *such a way* that everything about them must be treated by exhibiting directly. Phenomenology is descriptive in its approach but its description is not the same as we find, say, in botanical morphology. Phenomenological description avoids characterizing anything without a direct demonstration. Description by direct demonstration means establishing the object of description in terms of its 'thinghood' (*Sachheit*). It means giving it a scientific definiteness as we encounter it phenomenally. Phenomenology takes into its grasp only that which demands to become a phenomenon. It grasps the phenomenon in terms of its ownmost content as a thing. That is, it grasps the phenomenon thematically as its object. What it grasps is not just this or that entity but the Being of entities which has been forgotten (*BT* 59).

Heidegger holds that phenomenology is a method of access to what is to be the theme of ontology. It is a way of demonstrating precisely the theme of ontology. That is why, it is "only as phenomenology, is ontology possible" (*BT* 60), says Heidegger. In phenomenology, the phenomenon comprises the Being of entities, its meaning, its modifications and derivatives. The Being of entities is not an appearing but that which shows itself. There is essentially nothing hidden behind the Being of entities; nor is there anything which does not appear behind it. But a phenomenon or rather what is to become a phenomenon can be hidden or not given. In other words, a phenomenon can also be covered-up. It is not the noumenon but covered-upness that is the counter-concept of phenomenon. A phenomenon may be covered up in several ways. It can be covered up in the sense that it is still *undiscovered*; it can be covered up in the sense that it is *buried over* (*Verschiittet*). Covering up of a phenomenon can also be in the sense of disguising wherein the possibilities of misleading are stubborn. And because the phenomena are covered up, there is a need for phenomenology.

Phenomenology is the way in which Being and its structures are encountered in the mode of phenomenon. It is explicating phenomena in an 'original' and 'intuitive' way. It is opposed to the *naiveté* of a haphazard, 'immediate' and unreflective 'beholding' (*Sachanen*). Phenomenology which must be secured from its own objects, not only shows an *access* to the phenomena but also works as the *point of departure* (*Ausgang*) for its analysis. Having thus delimited the preliminary conception of phenomenology, Heidegger differentiates the terms "phenomenal" and "phenomenological." "Phenomenal" means that which is given and explicable in the way the phenomenon is encountered. "Phenomenological" is everything which goes to make up the way of exhibiting, explicating and conceiving the phenomenon. Phenomena, as understood phenomenologically, are those which make up Being. Being always is the Being of some entity. So Being should be uncovered only by bringing forward the entities themselves. The entities must also show themselves with the kind of access which genuinely belongs to them. It is only then that "the ordinary conception of phenomenon becomes phenomenologically relevant" (*BT* 61).

In so far as its subject matter is concerned, phenomenology is ontology, the science of the Being of entities or beings. As ontology, phenomenology takes as its theme Dasein which is ontologico-ontically a distinctive entity. It is only by taking Dasein as its theme that phenomenology can confront the question of the meaning of Being in general. Heidegger holds that the phenomenological method of description is *interpretation.* It is through the interpretation that the authentic meaning as well as the basic structures of Being which Dasein itself possesses are made known to Dasein. That is why Heidegger calls the phenomenology of Dasein a *hermeneutic* in its primordial sense. The business of hermeneutic is interpreting the meaning of Being and the structures of Dasein. In doing so, the hermeneutic exhibits the horizon for a further ontological study of those entities which do not have the character of Dasein. It works out the conditions on which the possibility of any ontological investigation depends. It also works as an analytic of the existentiality of existence which Dasein possesses. Heidegger regards this as the primary meaning of phenomenology (*BW* 86).

The Being that phenomenology interprets is not a class or genus of entities. Its universality is beyond the category of genus. Although Being pertains to entities, its universality must be sought beyond an entity and its possible character. As Heidegger puts it, "*Being is the transcendens pure* and simple" (*BW* 86). So also every disclosure of Being is *transcendens*. And the knowledge of the disclosure of Being is transcendental. That is why phenomenological truth, namely, the disclosedness of Being is "veritas transcendentalis" (*BW* 87), declares Heidegger.

Heidegger is of the view that phenomenology and ontology are not two distinct philosophical disciplines. They together constitute a philosophy having phenomena as its object and its own way of treating it. Heidegger holds that philosophy itself is universal phenomenological ontology; it takes its departure from the hermeneutic of Dasein. As an analytic of existence, it works as a guide for all philosophical inquiry at the point where it arises and to which it returns. The essential characters of phenomenology do not lie in its *actuality* as a philosophical movement. We can understand phenomenology only by taking it as a possibility.[11] Heidegger says "Our elucidations of the preliminary concept of phenomenology show that what is essential to it does not consist in its *actuality* as a philosophical "movement." Higher than actuality stands *possibility*. We can understand phenomenology solely by seizing upon it as a possibility" (*BW* 87).

NOTES

1. The German term "Sein" generally means 'to be.' But the translators of Heidegger have chosen to render it as "Being" for linguistic and stylistic smoothness and convenience.
2. Martin Heidegger, *Being and Time*. Trans. John Macquarie & Edward Robinson, Oxford, Basil Blackwell, 1978, p. 2. Abbreviated *BT*.
3. Martin Heidegger, *Basic Writings*, Nine Key Essays, Plus the Introduction to *Being and Time*. Edited with General Introduction and Introduction to Each Selection by David Farrel Krell, Routledge & Kegan Paul, London, 1978, p. 45. Abbreviated *BW*.

4. The term "Seindes" has several renderings like 'being,' 'essent' or 'entity.' Because of its affinity to the Latin "ens" which means 'something that is' translators prefer to render it as 'entity.'
5. Since the rationalist school of Christian Wolff (1679-1754) the term "Dasein" has been widely used in German Philosophy to mean 'existence' or 'that it is' (Da-sein), as opposed to 'essence' or 'what it is' (*was-sein*) of a thing, state of affair, person, or God. The term connotes especially the existence of living creatures and most notably of human beings. Around 1860 Darwin's "struggle for life" was translated as *Kampf ums Dasein*. Heidegger thus stresses the word's primary nuance. For him Dasein is that kind of existence that is always involved in an understanding of its Being. It must never be confused with the existence of things that lie before us, on hand, or at hand as natural or cultural objects (*Vorhandenheit* or *Zuhandenheit*). In order to stress the special meaning of Dasein, Heidegger often hyphenates the word as Da-sein which means 'there being.' It connotes the openness to Being characteristic of human existence which is 'there' in the world. Thus the term "Dasein" or "Da-sein" is often translated as "existence" or "human existence."
6. The term "ontological" refers to the Being of beings (*onta*) as well as to any account of the Being of beings. It also refers to the content and method of the discipline which we traditionally call metaphysics. On the contrary the term "ontic" refers to a manner of dealing with beings without raising the ontological question of Being about them. Most disciplines, according to Heidegger, remain "ontic" in their treatment of beings. Phenomenological ontology alone deals with being in the manner of raising the question of the meaning of their Being.
7. Johnson J. Puthenpurackal, *Heidegger Through Authentic Totality to Total Authenticity—A Unitary Approach to his Thought in its two phases.* Leuven University Press, Belgium, 1987, p. 9.
8. Heidegger coins the term *existentielle* to designate the way Dasein in any given case actually exists by realizing or ignoring its various possibilities. One of those possibilities is to inquire into the *structure* of its life and possibilities. The kind of understanding thereby gained Heidegger calls *existenzial*. The nexus of such structures he

calls Existentialitat. The translators have rendered the term *existentielle* as "existentiell," *existenzial* as "existential" and *existentialitat"* as "existentiality." In the analytic of Dasein, the terms "existential" and "existentiell" respectively correspond to the terms "ontological" and "ontic."

9. Johnson J. Puthenpurackal, p. 11.
10. Heidegger uses "Destruktion" as the equivalent of the English "Destruction." By this he does not mean the total annihilation of the history of ontology. "Destruktion" does not signify "destruction" in the usual sense which the German word "Zerstorung" expresses. Heidegger uses "Destruktion" in a neutral, constructive meaning of it.
11. In this connection Heidegger admits his indebtedness to his teacher Edmund Husserl. He says that his phenomenological investigations would not have been possible without the foundations laid by Husserl in his *Logical Investigations*. He maintains that it is with *Logical Investigations* that phenomenology achieved a break through.

Chapter III

Dasein and Being-in-the-World

In the previous chapter we have observed that Dasein is an entity which, in its very Being, comports itself understandingly towards that very Being. This means that Dasein, unlike other beings, is a being that exists. Dasein exists mineness as its essential character. Dasein is an entity "which in each case I myself am."[1] Mineness necessarily belongs to Dasein since it is an existent. It is on the condition of mineness that Dasein exists in either of the two modes, namely, authenticity or inauthenticity. Dasein always exists in any one of these two modes. It is in either of these ways that Dasein's Being takes on a definite character. Otherwise Dasein remains to be a modally undifferentiated entity. Authenticity and inauthenticity are a priori grounded upon the state of Being which is *Being-in-the-world*. That is, Being-in-the-world constitutes the very Being of the entity of Dasein. Dasein cannot but occur except in the framework of an encompassing world. Dasein and the world are so intimately related that one is unintelligible without the other. "Both are what they are only in being related to one another."[2] Heidegger therefore says that a correct analytic of Dasein warrants a proper understanding and interpretation of Dasein's state of Being-in-the-world.

The expression "Being-in-the-world" stands for a unitary phenomenon. It is a holistic datum which cannot be broken up into its contents. Yet it may be said that it contains three constitutive items in its structure. They are: (A) In-the-World, (B) the entity which has Being-in-the-world as its way of being, and (C) being-in (*In-sein*) as such.[3]

A. In-the-World

Heidegger discusses the first item of Being-in-the-world, namely, 'in-the-world' under four main headings: (i) the idea of the worldhood of the world, (ii) environmentality and worldhood in general, (iii) Phenomenological ontology of worldhood and Descartes' interpretation of the world, and (iv) spatiality and Being-in-the-world.

(i) The Idea of the Worldhood of the World

According to Heidegger, the world is an important item of the structure of Being-in-the-world. He therefore first takes up the analytic of the idea of the worldhood of the world. The analytic involves a phenomenological description of the world. Describing the world as a phenomenon means to let us see what shows itself in entities within the world. It is not a mere enumeration of the worldly things or entities like houses, trees, people, mountains, stars and so on. It is not the depiction of the way such entities 'look'; it is not even giving an account of the occurrences that take place in them and with them. The occurrences or the activities constitute a description which is pre-phenomenological in nature. Pre-phenomenological description is confined to entities only. It is ontical and not ontological in character. It is not at all relevant to phenomenology which is a description of 'things' not as entities but as 'phenomena.' What phenomenology seeks is not description of the entities but their Being which is found in their phenomena. Phenomenon, according to Heidegger, is that which shows itself as Being and as a structure of Being. So phenomenological description of the world means "to exhibit the Being of those entities which are present-at-hand within the world, and to fix it in concepts which are categorical" (BT 91), says Heidegger.

According to Heidegger there are two kinds of entities in the world—things of nature and things invested with value. Things of nature are called substances and substantiality is the characteristic of their Being. It is upon this substantiality that everything relating to their inquiry is founded. Natural and mathematical sciences explicate the substantiality of the substances that constitute Nature. But Heidegger contends that their explication of Nature as such or its Things will never reach the phenomenon of the world because world is vaster than Nature and its Things: "Nature is itself an entity which is encountered within the world and which can be discovered in various ways and at various stages" (BT 92). Heidegger also maintains that even the explication of things invested with value will not reveal the phenomenon of the world as such, since they too are the entities 'within' the world. Things invested with value, like Things in nature or Nature as a whole, are encountered within the world only. But the only difference between the things invested with value and Things of Nature is that the former are those with which Dasein proximally and for the most part dwells. That is why they are capable of showing the 'world' more penetratingly than Things of Nature. Yet, they cannot show us the world as the phenomenon because it is on the background of the world that they too exist. So the worldhood of the world cannot be reached either through the Things of Nature or through the Things invested with value. Heidegger says, "Neither the ontical depiction of entities within-the-world nor the ontological interpretation of their Being is such as to reach the phenomenon of the world. In both of these ways of access to 'objective Being,' 'the world' has already been 'presupposed,' and indeed in various ways" (BT 92).

To Heidegger, worldhood of the world as such is neither the common world in which we are; nor is it the subjective world of a Dasein. Worldhood is an ontological concept which stands for one of the items of Being-in-the-world. Being-in-the-world is a way in which Dasein's character is defined existentially. So the worldhood itself is an *existentiale*. That is, ontologically, inquiry about the world involves the analytic of Dasein as a field for thematic study. The world is rather a characteristic of Dasein itself. Ontologically, 'world' is not a way of characterizing the entities which Dasein essentially is not. Investigation into the phenomenon of the world entails investigation into the avenue of entities within the world and the being which they possess, through the analytic of Dasein.[4]

Heidegger says that the word "world" is used in several ways. Firstly, the term "world" is used as an ontical concept. Here it signifies the totality of those entities which can be present at hand within the world. Secondly, "world" functions as an ontological term which signifies the being of the entities like people, houses, trees and so on. The term can be used for any realm which encompasses a multiplicity of entities. For example, one may talk of the world of mathematician wherein "world" signifies the realm of possible objects of mathematics. Thirdly,[5] "world" can be understood in another ontical sense. In this sense the world implies a realm wherein a factical Dasein as such can be said to 'live.' World here has a pre-ontological existential signification with different possibilities. It may either stand for the public we-world or for one's own closest domestic environment. Finally, the term "world" designates the ontologico-existentiell concept of worldhood. Here worldhood itself may have as its modes the structural wholes any special "worlds" may have at the time. But *worldhood* as such embraces in itself the a priori character of worldhood in general.[6]

(ii) Environmentality and Worldhood in General

Heidegger discusses this topic under the following heads: (a) the Being of entities encountered in the environment, (b) announcing of the worldly character of the environment in entities within the world, (c) references and assignment and (d) involvement, significance and the worldhood of the world.

(a) The Being of the Entities Encountered in the Environment

Heidegger says that in our environment there are entities which we encounter as being closest to us. Their Being can be exhibited phenomenologically by taking our everyday Being-in-the-world as our clue. Our everyday Being-in-the-world may also be called as our dealings in the world with entities within-the-world. These dealings manifest themselves in manifold ways of concern. The dealings are not a bare perceptual cognition but a concern "which manipulates things and puts them to use" (*BT* 95). Phenomenology deals with the Being of the entities which we encounter in such concern. Entities are the preliminary and accompanying theme of phenomenology. But its primary theme is the disclosure and explication of the Being of entities. Here the entities which are taken as the preliminary theme are those which show themselves in our concern with the environment. These entities are not the objects for knowing the 'world' theoretically. They are simply what get used, what get produced, and so forth. So the entities which we encounter in our concern with environment become the preliminary theme for the purview of 'knowing' which is phenomenological in character. This phenomenological knowing looks primarily towards Being. By taking Being as its theme, the phenomenological knowing takes these entities as its accompanying theme also. Therefore, phenomenological interpretation in this sense is not a way of knowing the characteristics of entities. It is rather "a determination of the structure of the Being which entities possess" (*BT* 96). As an investigation of Being, phenomenology also brings to completion the understanding of Being which already belongs to Dasein and which comes alive in any of its dealings with entities. Phenomenology does it autonomously and explicitly.

Heidegger says that the entities which serve phenomenologically as the preliminary theme are those which are used or which are to be found in the course of production. They become accessible when we put ourselves into the position of concerning ourselves with them. They come to light in our concernful dealings with them. The kind of Being which belongs to such concernful dealings is the way in which everyday Dasein always *is*. For instance, when I open the door I use the latch. Phenomenological access to these entities is possible only when we put aside all our interpretative tendencies. Our tendencies to interpret keep thrusting themselves upon us. They conceal the phenomenon of our concernful dealing with entities. They conceal even the very entities which are encountered by their own accord in our concern with them. Concern (*Besorgend)* is the type of relation Dasein has to entities encountered in circumspection."[7]

Heidegger says that the entities which we encounter in our concernful dealings are neither the Things of nature nor the things invested with value but *equipment*. Equipment is manifold; it may be equipment for writing, sewing, working, measurement, transportation and so on. Phenomenology has to exhibit the kind of Being which equipment possesses. Strictly speaking there is no such thing as equipment. There is only the Being of equipment. The Being of equipment means a totality of equipment. Equipment is essentially 'something in-order-to: "Every equipment has a purpose, an in-order-to be (*Um-zu*)."[8] And a totality of equipment is constituted by various ways of the 'in-order-to.' These ways of 'in-order-to' may be called as serviceability, conduciveness, usability and manipulability. In the 'on-order-to' there lies an assignment of something to something. There is a manifold of such assignments. Equipment entails equipmentality. Equipment is always in accordance with its equipmentality. It always takes place in terms of its belonging to other equipment. For instance, ink-stand, pen, ink, paper, blotting, pad, table, lamp, furniture, windows, doors, and room. These things never show themselves as they are for themselves. What we encounter here as closest to us is the room. We do not encounter the room as something 'between four walls' in a geometrical sense. Instead, we encounter it as equipment for residing. It is out of the room as equipment the 'arrangement' emerges. It is in this arrangement that any 'individual' item of equipment shows itself. So a totality of equipment is prior to an individual item of equipment. We discover the former before we discover the latter.[9]

Equipment possesses the Being which is known as manipulatability. That is, we can seize hold of it and use it, instead of just stare at it. In manipulating an equipment, a particular relationship to it becomes more primordial. The Being of manipulation which an equipment possesses is called readiness-to-hand (*Zuhandenheit*). Readiness-to-hand cannot be discovered if we just look at the outward appearance of Things. Theoretical perception of Things does not reveal their readiness-to-hand. It is only in our practical dealings with them that we encounter their character of readiness-to-hand. It is in manipulating them that they require their specific Thingly character. The readiness-to-hand (*Zuhanden*) is not grasped theoretically at all. It is grasped in the work towards which entities are used. The shoe which is to be produced is for wearing. The clock is manufactured for telling the time. When we make use of the clock-equipment, which is proximally and inconspicuously ready-to-hand, the environing Nature is ready-to-hand along with it. Readiness-to-hand is the way in which entities as they are in themselves are defined ontologico-categorically. As against the entities that are ready-to-hand, which are encountered as equipments (*Zeuge*), there are other kinds of entities that are encountered in theoretical cognition. Heidegger calls them present-at-hand (*Vorhanden*): "It is not a division made between two types of entities, rather it refers to a distinction in Dasein's way of 'viewing' the entities. When Dasein views with 'circumspection' (*Umsicht*), they show themselves as ready-to-hand equipments. When Dasein, on the other hand adopts an attitude of merely observing (*Hinschauen*) the very same entities appear as merely present-at-hand."[10]

(b) Announcing of the Worldly Character of the Environment in Entities within-the-world

Heidegger says that the world itself is not an entity with-in-world. Yet it is the world that determines the discovery of entities in their Being. Unless 'there is' a world, entities cannot be encountered. In the absence of the world, entities can not show themselves in their Being as entities. Even the entity called Dasein has a pre-ontological understanding of the world. That is, Dasein is ontically constituted by Being-in-the-world. So the world shows itself through the entities which are encountered with-in-the-world. We can have a pre-phenomenological glimpse of the phenomenon of the world. We always have a glimpse of it without having to take it as a theme for ontological interpretation. Dasein itself has a possibility of Being in which the worldhood of the entities with which it is concerned is lit up for it. In the range of its concernful absorption in equipmental ready-to-hand, Dasein has a possibility of Being in which the worldhood of those entities within-the-world with which it is concerned is revealed for it, along with those entities themselves. Heidegger wants to study the phenomenon of the possibilities of Being which Dasein has and in which the worldhood of the entities within-the-world is revealed in the concernful dealings of Dasein with them. He wants to highlight the structures which show themselves in the phenomenon of the worldhood.[11]

Being-in-the-world possesses the character of everydayness. The everydayness of being-in-the-world carries with it certain modes of concern with entities to be encountered in such a way that the worldly character of what is within-the-world comes to the fore. Heidegger classifies these modes as conspicuousness, obtrusiveness and obstinacy. Conspicuousness is discovered when an entity which is most closely ready-to-hand is met as something unusable. Obtrusiveness arises when something ready-to-hand is found missing. That which is ready-to-hand enters the mode of obtrusiveness when we notice what is unready-to-hand. And the mode of obstinacy is seen when anything which is missing or unready-to-hand is disturbing to us. Heidegger says that the modes of conspicuousness, obtrusiveness and obstinacy have the function of bringing to the fore the characteristic of presence-at-hand in what is ready-to-hand. The ready-to-hand is thus encountered through modifications in which its presence-at-hand is revealed. Heidegger opines that the analysis of these modifications does not fully clarify the phenomena of the world. The analysis does not take us beyond the Being of what is within-the-world. It does not take us closer to the world of phenomenon than before. Nevertheless, it brings us to a point where the phenomenon of the world is brought into our view.[12]

(c) Reference and Assignment

As it has been mentioned, the world is brought to light in certain definite ways in which we concern ourselves environmentally with the ready-to-hand. The world has been lit up only *with* the readiness-to-hand of that concern. Heidegger says that we have to proceed further in understanding the Being of entities within-the-world. The further we proceed in understanding the Being of entities within-the-world, the broader and firmer becomes the phenomenal basis on which the world-phenomenon is laid bare. So the Being of the ready-to-hand should be studied now with the purpose of grasping the phenomenon of *reference* or *assignment*. He attempts an ontological analysis of a kind of equipment in which we come across the phenomenon of references. He reveals the characterization of references through an elaborate interpretation of signs like an adjustable red arrow with which motor cars are sometimes fitted up. The arrow of the motor car, depending on its position, indicates the direction the vehicle will take at an intersection. As a sign, the arrow is an item of equipment which is ready-to-hand for the driver in his concern with driving. The arrow is made use of even by those who are not travelling with the driver. They make use of it either by giving way on the proper side or by stopping. The arrow is ready-to-hand within-the-world in the whole equipment-context of vehicles and traffic regulations. Heidegger says, "It is equipment for indicating, and as equipment, it is constituted by reference or assignment. It has the character of the 'in-order-to,' its own definite serviceability. It is for indicating. This indicating which the sign performs can be taken as a kind of 'referring'" (*BT* 109).

A sign is something ontically ready-to-hand. It functions both as the definite equipment and as something indicative of the ontological structure of readiness-to-hand. "Thus, sign as something ready-to-hand has a two-fold reference: a reference of indicating as *this* particular equipment, and also a reference indicative of the ontological structure of readiness-to-hand, of referential totalities and of worldhood."[13] The special status of the sign as something ready-to-hand is rooted in the environment with which we concern ourselves circumspectively. So the reference or assignment cannot be conceived as a sign. Reference only serves ontologically as the foundation upon which signs are based. It is not an ontical characteristic of something ready-to-hand. It is only that by which readiness-to-hand is constituted.

(d) Involvement, Significance & the *Worldhood of the World*

Further, Heidegger is of the view that the worldhood of the world is lit up by the structures like involvement and significance which are encountered in the readiness-to-hand. The readiness-to-hand is always encountered within-the-world. The Being of readiness-to-hand stands in some ontological relationship to the world and its worldhood. That is, in anything that is ready-to-hand the world is always 'there.' Whenever we encounter anything, the world has already been discovered. The world can also be lit up in certain ways of dealing with our environment. The world is that in terms of which the readiness-to-hand is readiness-to-hand. That is, what we encounter within-the-world has, in its very Being, been freed for our concernful dealings and circumspection. It means that what we encounter within-the-world has, as it were, been released or given free reign so that our dealings with it can take note of it. It means that what we encounter has been given its freedom or set free so that our circumspection can take account of it. This freeing of what we encounter is an ontologically distinctive feature of the world (*BT* 115).

As it has already been mentioned the Being of the ready-to-hand has the structure of assignment or reference. It means that the Being of ready-to-hand has in itself the character of *having been* assigned or referred (*Verwiesenheit*). An entity is discovered when it has been assigned or referred to something. Any such entity also has an involvement in something. Involvement is the characteristic of being which belongs to the ready-to-hand. Having an involvement means letting be involved in something. Involvement is the Being of an entity within-the-world which has been proximally freed for its Being. An entity as an entity must have some involvement or the other. Having such an involvement is ontologically a definite structure of the Being of such an entity: "Ontologically letting entities be involved means disclosing the totality of involvements as the world within which entities may be involved.[14]

Involvement is not an ontical assertion about an entity. For instance, the hammer, which is ready-to-hand has an involvement in making something fast; with making something fast, there is an involvement in protection against bad weather; and this protection 'is' for the sake of providing shelter for Dasein; it is for the sake of a possibility of Dasein's Being. Thus there is a totality of involvements for anything that is ready-to-hand.[15] The totality of involvements goes back ultimately to a 'towards-which' of serviceability in which an entity is involved. Here the 'towards-which' of an entity which is ready-to-hand is not an entity with the kind of Being that belongs to what is ready-to-hand within the world; it is rather an entity whose Being is defined as Being-in-the-world; it is to this state of Being that worldhood itself belongs; it is the 'towards-which' in which there is no further involvement. Heidegger says, "This primary 'towards-which' is not just another 'towards-this' as something in which an involvement is possible. The primary 'towards-which' is a 'for-the-sake-of-which.' But the 'for-the-sake-of which' always pertains to the Being of Dasein, for which, in its Being, that very Being is essentially an issue" (*BT* 117). Thus Heidegger shows the interconnection by which the structure of an involvement leads to Dasein's very Being as the sole authentic 'for-the-sake-of which.'

Involvement is the Being of something ready-to-hand. It is discovered only on the basis of the prior discovery of a totality of involvements. In any involvement that has been discovered, the worldly character of the ready-to-hand has been discovered before hand. It is in the totality of involvements that there is an ontological relationship to the world. The other structure through which the world and worldhood are sought is significance. Significance is the relational totality constituted by Dasein in its understanding of assignments. Dasein's understanding of an entity as ready-to-hand lets itself reveal assignments in the relationships. The relational character which the relationships of assigning possess is called signifying. Dasein is always in familiarity with these relationships of assignment. It is by being familiar with them that Dasein gives both its Being and its potentiality-for-Being as something which it has to understand with regard to its Being-in-the-world. The relationships of assignment are as follows: 'a for-the-sake of which,' an 'in-order-to,' a 'towards-this,' an 'in which' of letting something be involved and the 'with-which' of an involvement. Each one of them signifies the succeeding one. These relationships are bound up with one another as a primordial totality. They are what they are as this signifying (*Be-deuten*) in which Dasein gives itself beforehand its Being-in-the-world as something to be understood: "The relational totality of this signifying we call 'significance.' This is what makes up the structure of the world—the structure of that wherein Dasein as such already is" (*BT* 119), says Heidegger.

Dasein is primordially in familiarity with significance. Dasein's familiarity with significance is the ontical condition for the possibility of discovering entities in a world with involvement as their kind of Being. It is through this familiarity that entities can make themselves known as they are in themselves (*in seinem an-sich*). Dasein is always such an entity that along with its Being, a context of the ready-to-hand is already and essentially discovered. That is, Dasein has always submitted itself to a world which it encounters. Dasein is not only familiar with significance, but also understands and interprets it. In doing so Dasein discloses such things as 'significations.' The significance thus disclosed is precisely the existential state of Dasein. That is, the disclosed significance is nothing but the Dasein's state of Being-in-the-world. It is also the ontical condition for the possibility that a totality of involvements can be discovered. Whereas Dasein's disclosure—understanding and interpretation—of significance is the ontological condition which makes it possible for Dasein to disclose it. Thus the worldhood of the world is the Being of that ontical condition which makes it possible for entities within-the-world to be discovered at all. The Being of the worldhood of the world gives us an *existential* way of determining the nature of Being-in-the world of Dasein. Besides the Being of the worldhood of the world, there are two other kinds of Being, viz., readiness-to-hand and presence at-hand. The Being of readiness-to-hand is the Being of those entities within-the-world which we proximally encounter. And the Being of presence-at-hand is the Being of those entities which we can come across and whose nature we can determine by going through the entities proximally encountered. Unlike the Being of the worldhood of the world, the Being of these two entities is categorical. It is different from the kind of Being which Dasein possesses.

Heidegger contends that the system of relations of assignment which constitute the worldhood of the world does not volatilize the 'substantial Being' of entities within-the-world into a system of relations. The system does not dissolve the Being of entities into pure thinking inasmuch as relations are always something thought. On the contrary, the system of relations provides the basis on which "the entities can for the first time be discovered as they are 'substantiality' in themselves" (*BT* 122).

In the proceeding analyses Heidegger has tried to lay bare the horizon within which the worldhood of the world is to be sought. He has only touched upon the ontological context of Dasein's assigning itself with the entities within-the-world. Heidegger attempts a further clarification of worldhood by making a contrast between his analysis of worldhood and Descartes' interpretation of the world. He tries to bring out the specifically ontological problematic of worldhood more sharply by examining Descartes' ontology of the world.

(iii) Phenomenological Analysis of Worldhood and Descartes' Interpretation of the World

Heidegger says that Descartes' ontology of the world is founded on the concept of extension. Spatiality, which Descartes identifies with extension, constitutes the world. He defines the world in terms of the reality that extends. The ontological grounds for defining the world as *res extensa* lie in the idea of substantiality. But Heidegger contends that Descartes has failed to clarify the meaning of the Being of substantiality. Descartes treats the idea of substantiality as something incapable of clarification. He only considers substantiality as the property of a particular substance. Since Descartes mistook it to be self-evident, its meaning remains to be unclarified. Heidegger says, "Descartes not only evades the ontological question of substantiality altogether; he also emphasizes explicitly that substance as such—that is to say, its substantiality—is in and for itself inaccessible from the outset" (*BT* 126).

Heidegger further says that Descartes' ontology of the world does not seek the phenomena of the world at all. It does not even define any entity within-the-world fully enough so that the worldly character of this entity is fully revealed. The entity which Descartes tries to grasp through his idea of extension is Nature and not the world. But in fact, Nature, according to Heidegger, is only an entity within-the-world. Nature cannot be equated with the world. Descartes has mistaken the world for Nature. His conception of the world is defective, since the foundations on which it is based have led him to be oblivious of the phenomenon of the world. His interpretation of the world fails to analyse the Being of those entities within-the-world which are proximally ready-to-hand. Heidegger holds that Descartes' ontology of the world is not mathematical in spirit. It is not determined by the science of mathematics which he esteems very highly. It is so because Descartes does not let the entities within-the-world to present the kind of Being which belongs to them. Instead, he prescribes for the world its 'real' Being, as it were, on the basis of an idea of Being whose source has not been disclosed. Descartes has completely ignored the idea of Being which has to be demonstrated in its own right. He has neglected the idea of Being in which Being is equated with constant presence-at-hand. Descartes failed to raise the equation of how to appropriate access to entities within-the-world. Obtaining proper access to the phenomenon of the world is an important step in Heidegger's exposition of the problem of the world. Unable to obtain access to entities within-the-world, Descartes has mistakenly identified entities within-the-world with world in general. He has failed to bring Dasein's ways of behaving into view in an appropriate manner. He has mistaken the Being of Dasein to be a substance. He has treated it in the very same way as he has treated the Being of the *res extensa*. He is unaware of the mode of Being-in-the-world which belongs to the Being of Dasein. Since he knows no such thing as within-the-worldness he also knows no such thing as the phenomenon of the world. Heidegger writes: "By taking his basic ontological orientation from traditional sources and not subjecting it to positive criticism he [Descartes] has made it impossible to lay bare any primordial ontological problematic of Dasein; this has made it inevitable for the ontology of the 'world' to be compressed into that of certain entities within-the-world" (*BT* 131).

(iv) Spatiality and Being-in-the-World

As against Descartes who has tried to interpret the world in terms of extension, Heidegger attempts an interpretation of the world in terms of space. Heidegger says that the world is spatially determined in three ways: (1) by the spatiality of the ready-to-hand within the world, (2) by the spatiality of Being-in-the-world and (3) by the spatiality of Dasein.

Heidegger says that what is ready-to-hand is in space within-the-world. The Being of what is ready-to-hand is within space. The phenomenon of spatiality is bound up with the structure of Being which belongs to the ready-to-hand. Ready-to-hand means the entities which we encounter proximally or which we encounter *first* before any others. It also means the entities which are 'close by.' That is, what is ready-to-hand has the character of *closeness*. This closeness is inherent to what is ready-to-hand. It regulates itself in terms of calculative use. It gets established by the circumspection of concern and by the direction in which the ready-to-hand is accessible. Thus the closeness of what is ready-to-hand is given directionality. It shows that the ready-to-hand has its position in space as present-at-hand somewhere. That is, the ready-to-hand as equipment has its place (*platz*). This place defines itself as the place of this equipment. In each case the place is the definite 'there' or 'yonder' (*Dart und Da*) of an item of equipment which belongs somewhere. The place has the character of belonging-somewhere which corresponds to equipmental character of what is ready-to-hand. It also corresponds to the belonging-to which the ready-to-hand has towards a totality of equipment. There is also what is known as the "whither" which is the underlying condition which makes possible the belonging-somewhere of an equipmental totality as something that can be placed. We keep the "whither" circumspectively in view in our concernful dealings. This "whither" Heidegger calls *region* (*BT* 136). Thus the worldhood of the world is revealed through the structures of closeness, position, place and region through which the ready-to-hand is encountered.

Just as the spatiality of the ready-to-hand, the spatiality of Being-in-the-world also reveals the world. Being-in-the-world implies that Dasein is a Being of spatiality. Dasein is 'in' the world in the sense that it deals with entities encountered within-the-world. Dasein's spatiality is endowed with the characters of de-severance and directionality. De-severance is a kind of Being which Dasein has with regard to its Being-in-the-world. It implies a signification which is both active and transitive. It stands for a constitutive state of Dasein's Being. It amounts to making the farness vanish. That is, it means making the remoteness of something disappear and bringing it close. Dasein is essentially de-severant; it lets an entity be encountered close by as the entity which it is: "In Dasein there lies an essential tendency towards closeness. All the ways in which we speed things up, as we are more or less compelled to do today, push us on towards the conquest of remoteness. With the radio, for example, Dasein has so expanded its everyday environment that it has accomplished de severance of the world." (*BT* 140)

As Dasein is essentially spatial in the way of de-severance, Dasein has likewise the character of directionality. Every de-severances or bringing-close (*naherung*) takes in advance a direction towards a region out of which what is de-severed brings itself close. Directionality is given by the circumspective concern which is de-severing. Dasein constantly takes directions along with it, just as it does its de-severances. Dasein's spatialization is marked out in accordance with these directions. The directionality which belongs to de-severances is founded upon Being-in-the-world. De-severance and directionality are the constitutive characteristics of Being-in. They are determinative for Dasein's spatiality. They are the bases of Dasein's being in space concernfully and circumspectively. They are responsible for Dasein's being in space within-the-world. Thus Dasein's Being-in-the-world in the modes of de-severance and directionality reveal the phenomenon of the world.[16]

Thirdly, the phenomenon of the world is revealed by the spatiality of Dasein also. Dasein's circumspective and concernful Being-in-the-world is always spatial. Dasein is spatial in the way of de-severance and directionality. It is through Dasein's de-severance and directionality that what is ready-to-hand within the world is encountered in its spatiality. Dasein lets entities be encountered in the way which is constitutive for Being-in-the-world. In doing so, it gives them space or makes room for them. Giving space or giving room for entities belongs to its Being-in-the-world. It is with Being-in-the-world that space is proximally discovered in the spatiality. It is on the basis of the spatiality thus discovered that space itself becomes accessible for cognition. Thus the phenomenon of space is exhibited by Dasein's Being-in-the-world and the Being of the entities within-the-world. Space is necessarily founded upon the world, "Unless we go back to the world, space cannot be conceived. Space becomes accessible only if the environment is deprived of its worldhood; and spatiality is not discoverable at all except on the basis of the world. Indeed space is still one of the things that is constitutive for the world, just as Dasein's own spatiality is essential to its basic state of Being-in-the-world" (*BT* 148).

B. The Entity which has Being-in-the-World as its way of Being

So far we have presented Heidegger's analysis of the first constituent item, namely, in-the-world, of Being-in-the-world. We have inquired into the ontological structure of the world. We have also defined the idea of worldhood as such by viewing the phenomenon of the ready-to-hand in its various dimensions. We have interpreted the world ontologically by going through what is ready-to-hand within-the-world. Our task now is to analyse the second item, namely, the *entity* which in every case has Being-in-the-world as the way in which it is. This requires the explanation of *that* which one inquires into when one asks the question 'who?' We have to phenomenologically demonstrate and determine 'who' is in the mode of Dasein's average everydayness. To accomplish this task we have to study certain structures of Dasein which are equiprimordial with Being-in-the-world. The structures are as follows: being-with (*Mitsein*), Dasein-with (*Mitdasein*) and Being-one's-self (*Salbstein*). Heidegger discusses these modes under three headings: (i) the existential question of the "who" of Dasein; (ii) Dasein-with of Others and everyday Being-with, and (iii) Dasein's everyday Being-one's-Self and the "they."

(i) The Existential Question of the "who" of Dasein

This section constitutes giving an answer to the question—who the average Dasein is? Dasein may be defined as an entity which is in each case I myself. Its Being is in each case mine. This definition merely indicates an ontologically constitutive state of Dasein. It also tells us that ontically Dasein is in each case "I" and not Others. The answer to the question who the Dasein is, is inherent in the question itself. The answer is the "I," the 'Subject' or the 'Self.' The "who" maintains itself as something identical throughout the changes in its experiences. It relates itself to the changing multiplicity. Ontologically it is something which is in each case already and constantly present-at-hand. It lies at the basis of all changes as the *subjectum.* It is something which is selfsame in manifold otherness. Thus the "who" has the character of the *Self.* The *Self* is not the soul substance; nor is it the Thinghood of consciousness. But it implies something whose Being carries the meaning of present-at-hand. It implies an entity which is substantial in nature. This is none other than Dasein itself. The "I" or the *Self* discloses Dasein in its everydayness. Access to Dasein is gained through the reflective awareness of the "I" of actions. Thus the givenness or the present-at-hand of the "I" leads to Dasein. Dasein is in each case mine and this is its constitution. And that is the reason why Dasein is *not itself*, proximally and for the most part. The "I" is an essential characteristic of Dasein. Dasein's essence is grounded in its existence. Dasein's essence, its "I" must be interpreted existentially. That is, the "who?" is to be answered by exhibiting phenomenally as a definite kind of Being which Dasein possesses. In each case Dasein is its Self only in existing. Dasein cannot stand by itself; it can exist only as the Self in constancy. Self is the only way of the Being of Dasein. This does not tantamount to volatilizing the real 'core' of Dasein. The idea of the volatile core of the Dasein is based on the wrong assumption that Dasein has the kind of Being which belongs to something present-at-hand but without the solidity of a corporeal thing which occurs in the world. Dasein or man is a 'substance' which is *existence*; it is not a spirit which is a synthesis of soul and body (*BT* 152-53).

(ii) Dasein-with Others and Everyday Being-with

Heidegger says that a bare subject without a world is never given. An isolated "I" without the Others is far from being given. In Being-in-the-world, the Others are already there with us (*mit da sind*). Similarly any entity that is ready-to-hand refers to Others. For example, when one is at work, those Others for whom the 'work' is destined are encountered too. Similarly, when a material is put to use, we encounter its producer or supplier. The book we have used was bought at so-and-so's shop and given by such-and-such a person and so forth. Thus every entity that is ready-to-hand is indicative of Others. Others are encountered in any environmental context of equipment: "The boat anchored at the shore is assigned in its Being-in-itself to an acquaintance who undertakes voyages with it; but if it is a boat which is strange to us, it still is indicative of Others" (*BT* 154). Heidegger says that the Others are not somehow added on in thought to some Thing which is present-at-hand. Things are encountered as they are ready-to-hand for Others. They are encountered for Others in a world which is always mine too. Thus the entities have a character other than that of Dasein. By 'Others,' Heidegger does not mean everyone else but me. Others are not those over and against whom the "I" stands out: "They are rather those from whom, for the most part, one does *not* distinguish oneself those among whom one is too" (*BT* 154). Others are the entities which also are 'in' the world; they are also encountered within-the-world. They are 'in' the world by way of Being-in-the-world. They are neither present-at-hand nor ready-to-hand. On the contrary, Others are *like* the very Dasein which frees them. In that *they are there too*, and *they are there-with Dasein*. Here the 'too' means a sameness of Being as circumspectively concernful Being-in-the-world. The 'with' is something of the character of Dasein. This shows that the world is always the one that I share with Others: "The world of Dasein is a with-world (*Mitwelt*). Being-in is Being-with Others. Their Being-in-themselves within-the-world is Dasein-with (*Mitdasein*)."[17]

Others are encountered from out of the *world* in which circumspective Dasein dwells essentially and concernfully. Others are encountered *environmentally*. That is, Others are not encountered as human-Things present-at-hand. Instead, they are met 'at work,' and primarily in their Being-in-the-world. Even if we see the Others as 'standing around,' he or she is not apprehended as a person-Thing but as standing around in an existential mode of Being: "The Other is encountered in his Dasein-with in the world" (*BT* 156). The term "Dasein-with" designates that Being for which the Others who are freed within-the-world. The Dasein-with of Others is disclosed for a Dasein within-the-world. It is also disclosed for those who Dasein is with (*die Mit-daseienden*). This is possible because Dasein in itself is essentially Being-with. The assertion that "Dasein is essentially Being-with" is phenomenological in nature. It has an existential-ontological meaning. It means that the attribute of Being-with comes to Dasein from its own kind of Being. It does not come to it by reason of the occurrence of Others. Dasein carries the characteristic of Being-with even when factically no Other is perceived. It exists in the mode of Being-with although the Other is not present-at-hand: "Even Dasein's being-alone is Being-with in the world. The Other can be missing only in and for a Being-with. Being-alone is a deficient mode of Being-with; its very possibility is the proof of this" (*BT* 156-57).

Heidegger says that Dasein as Being-with comports itself towards Others who are themselves Dasein. Others are objects of *solicitude* (*Fursorge*) and not of concern. Concern, like Being-with, is a *Being towards* entities encountered within-the-world. Concern is also a form of solicitude. But solicitude is Dasein's Being-with Others. It is grounded in Dasein's state of Being as being-with. Being for, being against, being without one another, passing one another by and not mattering to one another are the possible ways of solicitude. Heidegger calls them deficient or negative modes of solicitude. They characterize the everyday and average being-with-one-another. They signify indifferent mode of solicitude. "The negative mode of solicitude is called 'indifference which is to be taken, not for the way in which the entities at random occur together, but for the way in which persons who are together do not matter to one another."[18]

In its positive sense, solicitude has two extreme possibilities. The first possibility is that in which solicitude takes away 'care' from the Other and puts itself in his position in concern. That is, solicitude can *leap in* for him. Here solicitude takes the Other over for that with which he is to concern himself. The Other is thrown out of his position and made dominated and dependent. This kind of solicitude is not only determinative of being with one another; it also pertains for the most part to our concern with the ready-to-hand. The other possibility of solicitude is that which does not so much leap in for Other as it leaps ahead of him in his existentiell potentiality-for-Being. It leaps ahead of the Other not to take away his 'care' but to give it back to him authentically. This kind of solicitude relates essentially to authentic care of the existence of the Other. It does not pertain to a "*what*" with which the Other is concerned. It helps the Other to become transparent to himself *in* his care and to become free for it. Everyday Being-with-one-another manifests itself between these two extremes of positive solicitude—that which leaps in and dominates the Other, and that which leaps forth and liberates (*vorspringend-be frienden*) the Other.[19]

The above analysis shows that Being with Others belongs to the Being of Dasein which is an issue for Dasein in its very Being. As Being-with, Dasein 'is' essentially for the sake of Others. In Being-with, Dasein is the existential for-the-sake-of Others. Even if a particular Dasein supposes that it has no need of Others, it can do so only in the mode of Being-with-Others who have been already disclosed in their Dasein. With their Being-with, Others' disclosedness has been constituted beforehand. This disclosedness makes up the worldhood which is tied up with the existential "for-the-sake-of-which." The worldhood of the world is such that there is essentially and already Dasein in it. The worldhood lets us encounter what is environmentally ready-to-hand as something with which we are circumspectively concerned. It does so in such a way that together with it we encounter the Dasein-with of Others. The structure of the worldhood is such that Others are not proximally present-at-hand as free-floating subjects along with other Things. In the world, Others show themselves in their special environmental Being. They do so in terms of what is ready-to-hand in that world (*BT* 160).

(iii) Dasein's Everyday Being-one's Self and the "They"

Ontologically, the 'subject' of any Dasein, either one's own or that of Others, has to be defined existentially. That is, it has to be defined in terms of certain ways in which one may be. In our concern with something, Others too are encountered as what they are and as what they do. Heidegger says that in Being-with-one-another, there is *distantiality* (*Abstandigkeit*) in it. The distantiality belongs to Dasein's Being-with. It keeps Dasein as everyday Being-with-one-another in *subjection (Botmassigkeit)* to Others. Here, Dasein 'ceases' to be itself and its Being is taken away by the Others. Dasein's everyday possibilities of Being are for Others to dispose off as they please. These others are not *definite* Others. Any Other can represent all Others who inconspicuously dominate the Dasein's Being-with. Here one belongs to the Other's oneself and enhances their power. We designate the Others only to cover up the fact that one's belonging to Others is essentially oneself. The Others are those who proximally and for the most part *are there* in everyday Being-with-one-another. These Others are neither oneself nor some people, nor the sum of them all. They are the "they" (*das Man*). "They" is the Being of Dasein's everyday being-with-one-another wherein Dasein is not itself. Here one's own Dasein is dissolved into the kind of Being of the Others. The 'they' dictates one's Dasein. We take pleasure as *they* take pleasure; we see and judge things as *they* do; we find shocking what *they* find shocking. The "they," which is nothing definite, and which all are, though not as the sum, "prescribes the kind of being of everydayness" (*BT* 164).

Averageness is an existential characteristic of the "they." The "they" maintains itself factically in the averageness of that which belongs to it. It is with this averageness that the "they" suppresses every kind of priority. In averageness, everything that is primordial gets glossed over as something that is well known. Everything gained by a struggle becomes just something to be manipulated. Every secret loses its force. Heidegger says, "This case of averageness reveals in turn an essential tendency of Dasein which we call the "levelling down" (*Einebnung*) of all possibilities of Being" (*BT* 165). Distantiality, averageness and levelling down are the ways of Being for the "they." These modes constitute what we know as publicness (*die Offentlichkeit*). Publicness controls every way of Dasein and the world. It even gets them interpreted. But the interpretation never gets to the heart of the matter. Publicness gets everything obscured and covered up. It treats everything as something familiar and accessible to all. Heidegger maintains that these modes of Being—everyday being-among-one-another, distantiality, averageness levelling down and publicness—represent Dasein's way of being as inauthenticity and failure to stand by itself. Inauthenticity is a mode wherein neither the self of one's own Dasein nor the Self of the Other has yet found itself or lost itself. Inauthenticity stands for Dasein's everyday self which is the *they-self.* This has to be distinguished from the *authentic self* which has been taken hold of in its own way (*eigens ergriffenen*). Whereas the inauthentic Self is that wherein the particular Dasein has been *dispersed* into the "they."

C. Being-in as Such

We have so far analysed the two structural items of Being-in-the-world which is the basic state of Dasein. The two items are (1) in-the-world, and (2) the entity which has Being-in-the-world as its way of being. Our task now is to analyse the third item of Being-in-the-world, namely, Being-in as such. We have to present Heidegger's interpretation of the phenomenon of Being-in, keeping in view the concrete analysis of the world and the entity which has Being-in-the-world as the way in which it is. An interpretation of this phenomenon gives us a complete phenomenological view of the structural whole of Being-in-the world. It will also pave a way to grasping the primordial Being of Dasein, namely, care.

According to Heidegger, Being-in is a Dasein's state which is an existentiale. Being-in does not mean the kind of Being which an entity has when it is in another entity, like water is in the glass, the garment is 'in' the cupboard, the bench is in the lecture room. It does not have a spatial 'in-one-another-ness' of things present-at-hand. Here the word 'in' does not signify a special relationship of one entity being in another. Instead, it means "to reside" (*innam*) or "to dwell" (*habitare*). In this sense the entity to which Being-in belongs is one which is in every case I myself am (*bin*). I reside or I dwell alongside the world as that which is familiar to me in such and such a way. The term "Being-in" signifies 'to reside alongside' and 'to be familiar with.' As Heidegger puts, "Being-in is thus the formal existential expression for the Being of Dasein, which has Being-in-the-world as its essential state" (*BT* 80).

'Being alongside' means being in the world in the sense of being absorbed in the world. This structure is an *existential* which is founded upon Being-in. 'Being alongside' the world never means Being-present-at-hand-together of things that occur. It does not mean being side-by-sideness of Dasein with the world. On the contrary, it means that Dasein is in the world in the mode of encountering the world. As an entity which is present-at-hand Dasein is ontologically entirely different from those entities whose present-at-hand is similar to factual occurrence of some kind of mineral. Dasein is such a kind of entity that it understands its ownmost Being in the sense of a certain factual Being of present-at-hand. But the factuality of the fact (*Tasache*) of Dasein's Being is ontologically different from the factual occurrence of a thing. It is as a Fact that there is Dasein. It is this Fact of Dasein's factuality that Heidegger calls facticity. "The concept of facticity implies that an entity within-the-world has Being-in-the-world in such a way that it can understand itself as bound up in its 'destiny' with the Being of those entities which it encounters within its own world" (*BT* 82).

Ontologically, there is a difference between Being-in as *existentiale* and Being-in as a category. The former belongs to Dasein which is being alongside other entity. The latter belongs to entities which are present-at-hand; it implies insideness which they can have with regard to one another. Dasein's being-in implies that it has an existential spatiality which is different from the spatiality of the things present-at-hand. Dasein's spatiality is possible only on the basis of Being-in-the-world in general. Dasein's Being-in-space cannot be explained by some ontical characterization.

As mentioned above, Dasein's Being-in is of the nature of facticity. Dasein's facticity is such that it disperses itself into several definite ways of Being-in. The multiplicity of these ways are: having to do with something, producing something, attending to something, making use of something, giving something up, undertaking, accomplishing, interrogating, considering, determining and so on. Heidegger says that all these ways have *concern* as their kind of Being. There are also other ways of concern like leaving undone, neglecting, renouncing, resting, etc. They are known as deficient modes of concern in which concern is a bare minimum. In its colloquial sense, "concern" may mean to carry out something. It can also mean to provide oneself with something. In an expression like "I am concerned for the success of the undertaking," the term "concern" may mean something like apprehensiveness. In contrast to its colloquial ontical sense,

Heidegger uses the expression "concern" as an ontological term for an *existentiale* which designates the Being of the possible ways of Being-in-the-world. Dasein's ways of concern are a testimony to the fact that it is also a Being of *care* (Sorge). Like concern, care is also an ontological structural concept. Care has nothing to do with tribulation, melancholy or the cares of life. Care is an existential character of Dasein. When ontologically understood, Dasein itself is care.[20] Heidegger discusses the structure of Being-in as such under three main headings: (i) Knowing the world, (ii) existential constitution of Being-there, and (iii) Dasein's everyday Being-there.

(i) Knowing the World

Being-in is not a property of Dasein which it sometimes has and sometimes does not have. Being-in is not an adventitious mode of Dasein. Dasein is never an entity free from Being-in. Dasein is essentially an entity with Being-in. It is because Dasein's Being is founded upon the existential state of Being-in that Dasein is able to discover the entities which it encounters environmentally. Encountering entities environmentally means knowing entities, availing oneself of them and so on. The phenomenon of Being-in is so fundamental that it gets 'seen' in a certain way in every Dasein. It thus gets seen because it constitutes the basic state of Dasein. It gets already disclosed for Dasein's understanding of Being itself. The structure of Being-in is always and in some way familiar both in and for Dasein. It is not only familiar but also known to Dasein. In this sense, *knowing* is the chief exemplification of 'soul's' relationship to the world. Knowing the world functions as the primary mode of Being-in-the-world. Relationship between world and soul is conceived as being grounded in these two entities themselves and in the meaning of their Being. Nothing is more obvious than that a 'subject' is related to an 'object' and vice versa. This state of Dasein's Being in which the subject and object are interrelated must be presupposed. It must be made an evident point of departure for analyzing the problems of epistemology as well as metaphysics. Relationship between the soul and the world means knowing the world. The phenomenon of Being-in is represented mostly by the example of knowing the world. Being-in-the-world must be exhibited more precisely with regard to knowing the world.[21]

As it has been mentioned, Being-in-the-world is a basic state of Dasein. In it Dasein operates in the mode of everydayness. So it is something which has always been experienced ontically and is never totally veiled from view. The very fact that Dasein has an understanding of its own Being implies that it always experiences Being-in-the-world. That is, Dasein is always in the mode of knowing the world. Knowing belongs solely to those entities which know, namely, human-subjects. Knowing is a mode of the Being of Dasein as Being-in-the-world. Ontically Dasein is founded upon the state of Being which is knowing. Knowing is not present-at-hand, it is not externally ascertainable as bodily properties are. Knowing possesses the characteristic of 'Being inside' (*innenseins*). Being inside does not refer to the subject's inside or its inner sphere as a sort of cabinet or box. It is difficult to give a positive interpretation of the Being-inside of the phenomenon of knowing grounded in the Being which belongs to the subject. It is also difficult to explain how knowing makes its way out of its Being inside and achieves transcendence towards its object. Knowing is a way of determining the nature of the present-at-hand by observing it. It implies that there is a deficiency in our having-to-do with the world concernfully. It is on the basis of perception and interpretation that knowing makes something determinate. What is thus made determinate can be expressed in propositions. It can be retained and preserved as what has been thus asserted. "This perceptive retention of an assertion about something is itself a way of Being-in-the-world" (*BT* 89).

In the process of knowing, Dasein does not get out of its inner sphere. Its primary kind of Being is such that it is always 'outside,' alongside entities which it encounters. When Dasein dwells alongside the entity to be known, there is no such thing as any inner sphere getting abandoned. Dasein remains to be still 'inside' even in its Being-alongside the object. Dasein is itself 'inside' as a Being-in-the-world which knows. Perceiving and knowing something is "not a process of returning with one's booty to the 'cabinet' of consciousness" (*BT* 89). Dasein which knows remains to be outside in all modes of knowing—perceiving, retaining and preserving. Even the modes of delusion, erring and forgetting must be conceived as a modification of the primordial Being-in which is constitutive of the phenomenon of knowing. The above analysis shows that the modes of Being-in-the-world which contribute to knowing the world are interconnected. It reveals that in knowing, Dasein achieves a new status of Being towards the world.

(ii) Existential Constitution of Being "there."

Further, Heidegger explicates Being-in as such in terms of the Being of the "there" which is the existential-ontological structure of Dasein. Dasein exists in such a way as to be its 'there.' By its very nature, Dasein brings its 'there' along with it. Dasein which lacks its 'there,' ceases to be Dasein. Dasein is essentially a Being which is its 'there.' That is why Heidegger calls Dasein a Being of *disclosedness*. Dasein is its disclosedness itself. It means that Dasein is 'illuminated' (*erleuchtet*) by and for itself. Being-in-the-world, Dasein is cleared (*gelichtet*) in itself. It is cleared not through any other entity except itself. It is cleared in such a way that it is itself the clearing. It is because Dasein is existentially cleared that the entities present-at-hand are accessible to it. It is because Dasein is its disclosedness that it is a Being which is an issue for it and it has to be its 'there' in its very Being. Let us now discuss the characteristics of Being-there through which Dasein discloses itself in its everyday manner.

(a) Being-there as State-of-mind and as Thrownness

According to Heidegger, state-of-mind is a fundamental *existentiale*. This phenomenon is the most familiar sort of thing like our mood or our being-attuned. In every case Dasein always has some mood (*gestimmt ist*). It is in the bad and pallid moods that Dasein becomes satiated with itself and its Being manifests as burden. These moods have a primordial disclosure. It is in this disclosure that Dasein is brought before its Being as 'there.' A mood of elation can alleviate the manifest burden of Being. The fact that a mood of elation is possible discloses the burdensome character of Dasein: "A mood makes manifest how one is and how one is faring (*wie einem ist und wird*). In this 'how one is,' having a mood brings Being to its 'there'" (*BT* 173).

In an ontico-existentiell sense, Dasein for the most part evades the Being which is disclosed in the mood. But in an ontologico-existential sense, even in such moods of evasion, Dasein is unveiled in its Being-Delivered-over to the "there." The fact that 'there' is something implies that it is disclosed. The characteristic of Dasein's Being, namely, 'that it is' is veiled in its 'whence' and 'whither.' In its being veiled, this characteristic is disclosed in itself. This is what Heidegger calls the 'thrownness' of Dasein into its 'there.' As Being-in-the-world, Dasein is thrown in such a way that it is the 'there.' 'Thrownness' discloses Dasein's state-of-mind 'that it is and has to be. The expression 'thrownness' is meant, as Heidegger puts it, "to suggest the facticity of its being discovered over" (*BT* 174).

Thrownness is the facticity of Dasein. It is an existential attribute of Dasein which has Being-in-the-world as its way of Being. It is not a property but a characteristic of Dasein's Being which is taken up into existence. Dasein is its 'there' in such a way that it finds itself (*sich befindet*) in its thrownness. That is, in a state of mind, Dasein is always brought before itself; it always finds itself but not in the sense of coming across itself by perceiving itself; it finds itself in the manner of being in the mood that it has. Dasein is an entity which has been delivered over to its Being. It is also delivered over to the fact that it must always have found itself. Its founding is not so much from a direct seeing as from fleeing. In its mood or state of mind, Dasein never looks at thrownness but it either turns towards or runs away from it. Its mood rarely turns towards its burdensome character of being thrown. But the thrownness of being 'there' with its 'that-it-is' stares in the face of Dasein. Thrownness remains to be an inexorability of an enigma to Dasein. Thus, mood discloses Dasein in its thrownness which Dasein can never overcome. So also Dasein can never go beyond its mood since the mood is its primordial kind of Being. Moods cannot be conquered by knowledge or will. They cannot be mastered by volition or cognition. Mood is prior to all cognition and volition. It is beyond the range of its disclosure. Moreover, a mood has to be mastered by another mood, a counter-mind. Dasein therefore can never be free of moods. Ontologically mood is Dasein's essential Being in which Dasein is disclosed to itself. "Ontologically, we thus obtain as the first essential characteristic of states-of-mind that *they* disclose Dasein in its thrownness and—proximally and for the most part—in the manner of an evasive turning-away" (*BT* 175).

(b) Fear as State-of-Mind

According to Heidegger, fear is one of the basic states of mind of Dasein. He analyses the phenomenon of fear from three points of view, namely, (1) that in the face of which we fear, (2) fearing, and (3) that about which we fear. These possible ways of looking at fear are interrelated and reveal the general structure of states-of-mind.

Firstly, that in the face of which we fear is the 'fearsome.' It is something which we encounter within-the-world. It may have either readiness-to-hand, presence-at-hand or Dasein-with as its kind of Being. These items can often be and for the most part be 'fearsome' and threatening. They have detrimentality as their kind of involvement. That which is detrimental has something queer about it. It is not yet within a striking distance, but it is coming close. It is in such a drawing-closeness, that the detrimentality radiates its threatening character. Something may be detrimental in the highest degree; it may even be coming constantly closer. But if it is still far off, its fearsomeness remains veiled. If that which is detrimental is close by, then it is threatening. It is threatening in the sense that it may or may not reach us. As it draws closer, the threat becomes more aggravated. Then we say that it is fearsome (*BT* 180).

Secondly, the phenomenon of fearing as such is freed and allowed to become as something of concern to us. In fearing, we do not first ascertain a future evil and later fear it. Neither does fearing first take note of what is drawing close and threatening. But fearing discovers what is drawing close before hand in its fearsomeness. In fearing fear can look at the fearsome explicitly and make it transparent to itself. It is the circumspection that sees the fearsome since it has fear as its state-of-mind. Fearing is a slumbering possibility of Being-in-the-world in a state-of-mind. In being so, it has already disclosed the world.

Thirdly, that about which we fear is, in fact, that which fear fears about. It is that very entity which is afraid, namely, Dasein. Dasein, to repeat, is an entity for which in its Being this very Being is an issue. It is only such an entity that can be afraid. Fear reveals Dasein in the Being of its 'there.' It does so in varying degrees of explicitness. Fearing also discloses Dasein as endangered and abandoned to itself. As Being-in-the-world, Dasein is in every case concernful-Being-alongside. It exists in terms of what is concerned with. When what is concerned with is endangered, then Being-alongside is threatened. "Fear discloses Dasein predominantly in a private way. It bewilders us and makes us 'lose our heads.' Fear closes off our endangered Being-in, and yet at the same time lets us see it, so that when the fear has subsided, Dasein must first find its way about again" (*BT* 181).

Fear can manifest as fear about Others or as fear for Others. (*Furchten fur sie*). Fearing for the Other does not take away his fear, because the Other, *for* whom we fear, need not fear at all on his part. It is only when the Other is *not* afraid that we fear *for* him. It is only when the Other regards recklessly what is threatening him that we fear most *for* him. Fearing-for is a way of having a co-state-of-mind with Others. It is not necessarily a being-afraid-with; it is not even a fearing-with-one-another. 'Fearing about' is being afraid-for-oneself. One can 'fear about' without 'being-afraid.' There may be variations in the constituents of the phenomenon of fear. There are different possibilities of Being in fearing. Being-close by belongs to the structure of the threatening as encounterable. Fear becomes *alarm* (*Erschrecken*) when something threatening breaks in suddenly upon concernful Being-in-the-world. Fear becomes *dread* (*Grauen)* when that which threatens has the character of being altogether unfamiliar. And fear becomes terror (*Enstetzen*) where that which threatens is laden with dread and encountered with the suddenness of the alarming. Besides these possibilities, there are other modifications of fear, like shyness, timidity, and becoming startled. All these modifications of fear are possibilities of having a state-of-mind. They point to the fact that Dasein as Being-in-the-world is fearful (*Furchtsam*). Heidegger points that fearfulness has to be understood as an existential possibility of Dasein's essential state-of-mind. It is not to be understood in its ontical sense of a factical individualized disposition (*BT* 182).

(c) Being-there as Understanding

Being-there is one of the existential structures of the state of mind. *Understanding* is an equiprimordial structure of the state-of-mind which constitutes the Being-there. Understanding is an intrinsic structure of the state-of-mind. It is a basic mode of Dasein's Being. It is a fundamental *existentiale* which is one of the constituents of the Being of 'there' in general. Ontically, understanding means 'being able to manage something' or 'being competent to do something.' Understanding is the kind of Being which Dasein has as a potentiality for-Being. This kind of Being lies existentially in understanding. Dasein possesses its competence for something as its Being-possible. Being-possible is an essential characteristic of Dasein. Possibility in a primordial existentiale of Dasein. It pertains to the ways of its solicitude for Others and the world. It also pertains to its potentiality-for-Being towards itself and for the sake of itself. Possibility is not the same as liberty of indifference. Possibility is Dasein's being-free for its ownmost potentiality-for-Being. Dasein's Being-possible is transparent to itself in different possible ways and degrees. Understanding is the Being of such potentiality-for-Being. It 'is' always with the Being of Dasein in the sense of its existence. Dasein is such a being that in every case it has understood or not understood that it is to be in this way or that. Dasein 'knows' what it is capable of. It knows what its potentiality-for-Being is capable of. Heidegger says that this kind of knowing does not arise from an immanent self-perception. In fact it belongs to the Being of the 'there' which is essentially understanding. Since, in understanding, Dasein is its 'there,' it can fail to recognize itself and go astray. Of course, Dasein has in every case already gone astray and failed to recognize itself since understanding is accompanied by a state-of-mind and existentially surrendered to thrownness. In its potentiality-for-Being Dasein is delivered over to the possibility of first finding itself again in all its possibilities. Heidegger says, "Understanding is the existential Being of Dasein's own potentiality-for-Being; and it is so in such a way that this Being discloses in itself what its Being is capable of" (*BT* 184).

Understanding has the existential structure of *projection.* Projection also always presses Dasein towards its possibilities. It discloses Dasein's essential dimension of Being-in-the-world. Dasein is thrown into the kind of Being called projecting. Projecting is not comporting oneself towards a plan that has been already thought out. On the contrary, Dasein has already projected itself and it is projecting as long as it exists. That is, Dasein always has understood itself and always will understand itself in terms of its possibilities. Understanding as projection is such that it throws before itself the possibility as possibility. It does not grasp its possibilities thematically. "As projecting, understanding is the kind of Being of Dasein in which it is its possibilities as possibilities" (*BT* 185).

Dasein is 'more' than what it factually is, since its Being is constituted by the *existentiale* of projection. But Dasein is never more than what it factically is, since its potentiality-for-Being belongs essentially to its facticity. Yet, Dasein is existentially that which it is *not yet.*

(d) Interpretation and Assertion

Heidegger says that the phenomenon of understanding develops itself into interpretation. As mentioned above, Dasein projects its Being upon possibilities. This Being-towards-possibilities is a potentiality for Being. It is so because of the way these possibilities exert their counter-thrust on Dasein. Thus, the projecting of the understanding has its own possibility of developing itself further. This development is 'interpretation.' In interpretation the understanding appropriates that which is understood by it. In it understanding does not become something different but it becomes itself. Interpretation is existentially grounded in understanding. Understanding does not arise from interpretation. Interpretation is not acquiring information about what is understood. On the contrary, interpretation is the working out of possibilities projected in understanding. In interpretation, we do not throw a 'signification' on something naked and present-at-hand. We do not stick a value on it. But when something is encountered as such, it has an involvement which is disclosed in our understanding of the world. This involvement is one which gets laid out by the interpretation. Interpretation is an appropriation of understanding. It operates in Being towards a totality of involvements which is already understood. It is grounded in something we see in advance or in a fore-sight. Interpretation reduces the entities into concepts to which it is opposed in its manner of Being. Interpretation decides in advance a definite way of conceiving an entity. It conceives an entity either with reservations or with finality. Interpretation is "grounded in something we grasp in advance—in a fore-conception" (*BT* 191).

Interpretation is founded not only on fore-conception but also on fore-sight and fore-having. It is never a presuppositionless apprehending of something. Anything interpreted has the 'as-structure' as its own, besides its connection with meaning. Meaning is that wherein the intelligibility (*Verstandlichkeit*) of something maintains itself. Meaning is that which can be articulated in a disclosure by which we understand. The concept of meaning encompasses the formal existential framework of what necessarily belongs to that which interpretation articulates. "Meaning is the 'upon-which' of a projection in terms of which something becomes intelligible as something; it gets its structure from a fore-having, a fore-sight, and a fore-conception" (*BT* 193). Understanding and interpretation are the existential states of Being of the "there." And meaning is the formal-existential framework of the disclosedness of understanding. Meaning is not a property of entities lying behind them. It is not something floating somewhere between Dasein and the entity. Meaning is an *existentiale* of Dasein. Dasein alone 'has' meaning and it alone can be meaningful (*sinnvolt*) or meaningless (*sinnlos*): "That is to say, its own Being and the entities disclosed with its

Being can be appropriated in understanding, or can remain relegated to non-understanding" (*BT* 193).

Heidegger's conception of meaning is in principle ontologico-existential. According to it, all entities other than Dasein must be conceived as *unmeaning* (*unsinniges*). They are essentially devoid of any meaning at all. Having no meaning does not mean having no value. Meaning here expresses only an ontological characteristic. That which is unmeaningful can also be absurd (*widersinning*). For instance, the natural events which Dasein encounters can assault its Being; they can break in upon us and destroy us.

Heidegger says that an interpretation is carried out in the form of assertion. Assertion is a derivating mode of interpretation. The term "assertion" signifies three meanings which are interconnected. Firstly, assertion signifies 'pointing out' (*Auf Zeigen*). It means letting an entity be seen from itself. For instance, in the assertion 'the hammer is too heavy,' what is discovered for sight is not a meaning, but an entity in the way that it is ready-to-hand. Secondly, assertion means 'predication.' In an assertion, we assert a predicate of a subject which is given a definite character (*bestimmt*) by the predicate. Here, what is put forward in the assertion is not the predicate, but the subject, say, the hammer itself. Thirdly, assertion means 'communication' (*Mitteilung*) or speaking forth (*Heraussage*). It is letting someone see with us what we have pointed out by way of giving it a definite character. It is sharing with the Other that entity which has been pointed out in its definite character. What is shared is our Being-towards what has been pointed out. It is a Being in which we see it in common. This Being-towards is Being-in-the-world. And what has been pointed out by the assertion gets encountered from out of this Being-in-the-world. In this sense an assertion is a communication in an existential sense (*BT* 196-97).

Heidegger holds that these three significations of assertion in their unity encompass the full structure of assertion. In its unified view, assertion may be defined as "pointing-out which gives something a definite character and which communicates" (*BT* 199). Assertion is not a free-floating kind of behaviour which might be capable of disclosing entities in general. On the contrary, assertion always maintains itself on the basis of Being-in-the-world. An assertion points out something by way of giving it a definite character. It is invariably related to an Articulation which is in accordance with significations or meanings. An assertion requires a fore-having of whatever has been disclosed by it. It requires a fore-sight. That is, an assertion operates with a definite way of conceiving. When an assertion is made, some fore-conception is already and always implied. This is evident in the following assertions like 'The hammer is heavy,' the hammer has the property of heaviness, and 'Heaviness belongs to the hammer.' "Like any interpretation whatever, assertion necessarily has a fore-having, a fore-sight and a fore-conception as its existential foundation" (*BT* 199).

(e) Discourse and Language

As it has been mentioned, the Being of 'there' or the disclosedness of Being-in-the-world is constituted by the fundamental existentialia comprising states-of mind and understanding. Understanding leads to interpretation which is an appropriation of what is understood. Interpretation leads to assertion which is a form of communication comprising 'saying' and 'speaking' which in turn give rise to discourse or talking. It is this discourse that is the existential-ontological foundation of language. Discourse is as primordial as state-of-mind and understanding. It underlies both interpretation and assertion. Discourse is the articulation of intelligibility. It is in language that discourse is expressed. Language is a totality of words. It is as the totality of words that discourse has a worldly Being of its own. This totality of words, namely, language, is an entity within-the-world. It is an entity which we come across as ready-to-hand. Language can be broken-up into word-Things which are present-at-hand. It articulates the disclosedness of an entity in terms of significations or meanings. It endows an entity with a Being which has been thrown and submitted to the world. Discourse is an existential state in which Dasein is disclosed. It is thus constitutive of Dasein's existence. Hearing and keeping silent (*Schweigen*) are the important possibilities of discourse. Discourse or talking is the way of articulating significantly the intelligibility of Being-in-the-world. Being-with belongs to Being-in-the-world which maintains itself in a definite way of concernful Being-with-one-another. The Being-with-one-another is always discursive which is either assenting or refuting, demanding or warning, pronouncing or interceding. The discursiveness of discourse may also be in the form of making assertion, talking in the way of giving a talk. Talking is a talk about something. What is talked about (*das Beredete*) in talk always talked to (*angeredet*) in a definite way and within certain limits: "In any talk or discourse, there is something said-in-the-talk as such (*ein Geredetes as solches*)—something said as such (*das . . . Gesagte als solches*) whenever one wishes, asks, or expresses oneself about something. In this 'something said,' discourse communicates" (*BT* 205). Communication is the articulation of Being with one another. A co-state-of-mind (*mitbe Findlichkeit*) gets shared through communication. The understanding of Being-with also gets shared through it. Communication is not a conveying of experiences like opinion or wish. In communication, there is no such thing as transferring of experiences from one's interior to another's interior. Communication is only a manifestation of Dasein-with as a co-state-of-mind and co-understanding.

The items that constitute discourse are as follows: (1) what the discourse is about; (2) what is said in the discourse as such; (3) the communication; and (4) the making-known. These items are the existential characteristics rooted in the state of Dasein's Being. They make language ontologically possible. It is only basing on these items that the essence of language is grasped. Discourse is constituted by both hearing and keeping silent. Hearing or listening to is Dasein's existential way of Being-open as Being-with for others. It constitutes the authentic way in which Dasein is open for its ownmost potentiality-for-Being. Dasein hears because it understands. Being-with develops in hearing—in listening—to one another (*Aufeinander-horen*). This listening can be done in several possible ways like following, going along with and not-hearing, resisting, defying, and turning away. Keeping silent is another possibility of discourse. It has the same existential foundation as hearing. In discourse the person who keeps silent can make one understand. He can do so more authentically than the person who talks more. Speaking at length is not a guarantee that understanding is deeper. Keeping silent is not the same as being dumb. A dumb person still has a tendency to 'speak.' Such a person has not proved that he can keep silent. Keeping silent authentically is possible only in a genuine discourse. It is only when Dasein has something to say that it is able to be silent. That is, it is only when Dasein has at its disposal a disclosedness of itself that it can be silent. This shows that Dasein can make something manifest even by being reticent. Being reticent means to do away with idle talk (*Gerede*). Reticence is a mode of discoursing, like talking. It articulates the intelligibility of Dasein in a primordial manner. Thereby it gives rise to a genuine potentiality for-hearing. It also generates a being-with-one-another which is transparent (*BT* 208).

(iii) Dasein's Everyday Being-There

Heidegger elaborates Dasein's everyday Being-there by explicating its constituent factors like (a) idle talk, (b) curiosity (c) ambiguity, and (d) falling.

(a) Idle Talk

Heidegger says that the phenomenon of idle talk does not signify something disparaging. On the contrary, it signifies a positive phenomenon that constitutes the Being of Dasein's understanding and interpreting. Idle talk is constituted by gossiping and passing the world along. It is a process of talking without proper grounds. It is a process which may ultimately end up in complete groundlessness (*Bodenlosigkeit*). Idle talk is not confined to vocal gossip. It even manifests in what we write. When writing takes the form of gossip, it becomes scribbling (*das Geschreibe*). In writing as scribbling the gossip is not based upon hearsay but upon superficial reading (*dem Angelesenen*). It takes place when the material is not drawn from primordial sources with a struggle. Despite being groundless, idle talk is public in nature. Idle talk is understanding everything without making it one's own. It can 'be raked up by anyone. It frees us from the trouble of genuine understanding. It develops an undifferentiated kind of intelligibility. Heidegger holds that discourse which constitutes Dasein's disclosedness, has the possibility of becoming idle talk. When discourse becomes idle talk it closes off the Being-in-the-world and covers up the entities within-the-world. In idle talk, one does not consciously pass off something as something else. Idle talk is only an act of closing off the world from an authentically articulated understanding. It discourages any new inquiry and disputation. It holds them back and suppresses them in a peculiar way. Idle talk is an everyday phenomenon. Interpreting things through idle talk is already established in Dasein. It is in the manner of idle talk that Dasein becomes acquainted with many things. Idle talk is an average understanding and interpretation of things. Dasein has grown into idle talk with a little possibility of extricating itself from it. Heidegger says that when Dasein maintains itself in idle talk "it is cut off from its primary and primordially genuine relationships-of-Being towards the world, towards Dasein-with and towards its very Being-in" (*BT* 214). In idle talk Dasein's understanding of itself gets uprooted. In it, Dasein keeps floating and yet it is always alongside the world, with Others and towards itself.

(b) Curiosity

Curiosity is Dasein's tendency towards seeing which belongs to its everydayness. Curiosity also expresses the tendency towards a peculiar way of letting the world be encountered in perception. Curiosity is concerned with seeing but without understanding. It is only concerned with leaping from novelty to novelty. In this kind of seeing that which is an issue for care lies an abandoning of oneself to the world. Heidegger characterizes curiosity to "be a specific way of not carrying along-side what is closest" (*BT* 216). So curiosity seeks restlessness and the excitement of changing encounters and continual novelty. Curiosity is concerned with the constant possibility of *distraction*. Curiosity is not interested in being damaged to the point of not understanding. It cannot observe entities and marvel at them. It concerns itself with a kind of knowing in order to have known. Besides *not-tarrying* in the environment with which one concerns oneself and the *distraction* by a new possibility, there is the third constituent item of curiosity, namely, the character of "never dwelling anywhere" (*Augenthaltslosigkait*). Therefore curiosity is of the nature of being nowhere and everywhere. As a mode of Being-in-the-world, curiosity reveals a new kind of the Being of Dasein in which it is constantly uprooting itself. Curiosity is intimately connected with idle talk in which each controls the other. They both have the tendency to uproot Dasein in its disclosedness. Heidegger says, "Curiosity, for which nothing is closed off, and idle talk, for which there is nothing that is not understood, provide themselves with the guarantee of a 'life' which, supposedly, is genuinely 'lively'" (*BT* 217).

(c) Ambiguity

The phenomena of idle talk and curiosity lead to another phenomenon, viz., ambiguity by which the disclosedness of everyday Dasein is characterized. Ambiguity is the phenomenon which we encounter in our everyday Being-with-one-another. It is accessible to everyone and about which anyone can say anything. It manifests even in Dasein's Being towards itself. It affects the way we avail ourselves of what is accessible for use and enjoyment; it affects the way we manage it. It establishes itself in the way Dasein projects itself and presents itself with possibilities. Ambiguity does not first arise from aiming explicitly at distortion and disguise. It is not something which the individual Dasein first conjures up. Ambiguity is already implied in Being-with one-another as *thrown* into the world. Ambiguity is the phenomenon wherein everything looks as if it were genuinely spoken, taken hold of and understood but at bottom it is not so. The way in which ambiguity presents Dasein's possibilities is heresy. Ambiguity persists in its understanding in the 'they.' It keeps the understanding constantly going wrong (*Versieht sich*) in its projects. In the public disclosedness of Being-with-one-another, Dasein is always ambiguously 'there.' Here, idle talk and curiosity keep things moving. As Heidegger puts it, "This ambiguity is always tossing to curiosity that which it seeks; and it gives idle talk the semi-balance of having everything decided in it" (*BT* 219).

(d) Falling

The phenomena of idle talk, curiosity and ambiguity are interconnected in their Being. They characterize the way in which Dasein is in its 'there.' That is, they characterize Dasein's disclosedness of Being-in-the-world. As definite existential characteristics, they contribute to making up of the Being of Dasein. They also reveal a basic kind of Being which belongs to the everydayness of Dasein's being. And it is this kind of Dasein's Being that Heidegger calls the *falling* of Dasein. Falling does not express a negative evaluation of Dasein. It only signifies that Dasein is *alongside* the world of its concern. Falling has the character of absorbing in and being lost in the publicness of the 'they.' In the first instance, Dasein has fallen away (*abge fallen*) from itself as an authentic potentiality for Being its self. It has also fallen into the world. "Fallenness into the world means an absorption in Being-with-one-another in so far as the latter is guided by idle talk, curiosity and ambiguity" (*BT* 220). Fallenness signifies the inauthenticity of Dasein. Inauthenticity signifies a kind of Being which is completely fascinated by the world and by the Dasein-with of others in the 'they.' Falling is a definite characteristic of Dasein itself. It is not a bad and deplorable ontical property but the ontologico-existential structure of Dasein. In falling, Dasein is something from which it has already fallen away. It has fallen into the world which belongs to its Being. Falling documents Dasein's existential mode of Being-in-the-world. Falling is effected by idle talk, curiosity and ambiguity. In idle talk, Dasein loses itself in the 'they' and falls to groundlessness. By resorting to idle talk "Dasein prepares for itself a constant temptation towards falling" (*BT* 221). This temptation is at the same tranquillizing which arises out of the supposition that all the possibilities of Dasein are secure, genuine and full. This supposition is developed by idle talk and ambiguity. The tranquillity marks Dasein's inauthentic Being. However, it does not seduce Dasein into stagnation and inactivity, but drives it into uninhibited 'hustle' (*Betriebs*). The tranquillization aggravates the falling.

Heidegger is of the view that falling is not only tempting and tranquillizing but also *alienating*. Here alienation does not mean that Dasein gets factically torn away from itself. But, alienation drives Dasein into a kind of Being which borders on the most exaggerated self-dissection. It closes off Dasein from its authenticity and possibility. It does not, however, surrender Dasein to an entity which Dasein itself is not. It only forces Dasein into its inauthenticity: "The alienation of falling—at once tempting and tranquillizing—leads by its own movement, to Dasein's getting *entangled* (*Verfangt*) in itself" (*BT* 223). Thus the phenomena of temptation, tranquillizing and alienation, and entanglement characterize Dasein's Being of falling. The movement of Dasein in this phenomenon is called the *downward plunge* of Dasein. In it Dasein plunges into the groundlessness and nullity of inauthentic everydayness. But this plunge remains hidden from Dasein by the way things have been interpreted publicly. Since, the plunge is of the inauthentic Being of the 'they,' it has a kind of motion which constantly tears the understanding away from the projecting of authentic possibilities. It leads the understanding into the tranquillized supposition that it possesses everything. It tears the understanding away from authenticity into the 'they.' The movement of falling is characterized by *turbulence* (*Wirbel*). The turbulence has the character of thrownness. Thrownness is neither a fact that is settled nor a fact that is finished. Thrownness belongs to Dasein, since it lets Dasein's facticity be seen phenomenally.

The phenomenon of falling does not go against the definition of Dasein as an entity for which, in its Being, its potentiality-for-Being is an issue. Dasein's falling does not preclude its existentiality that its Being is in the state of Being-in-the-world. Falling into the world does not mean that Dasein is an isolated "I" or Subject for which the world is an object. Dasein's falling is a Being-present-at-hand in the manner of an entity within-the-world. Falling is only a kind of the Being of Dasein's Being-in. In falling, what is at issue is our potentiality-for-Being-in-world in the mode of inauthenticity. It is only because Being-in-the-world is an issue for Dasein that Dasein falls. Falling does not give a 'night view' of Dasein but reveals its essential ontological structure: "Far from determining its nocturnal side, falling constitutes all Dasein's ways in their everydayness" (*BT* 224).

NOTES

1. Martin Heidegger, *Being and Time*. Trans. John Macquarie & Edward Robinson, Basil Blackwell, Oxford, London, 1978, p. 78.
2. Hebert Spiegelberg, *The Phenomenological Movement*, Vol. I. Martinus Nijhoff, The Hague, 1961, p. 328.
3. *Ibid.*, p. 329.
4. H.J. Blackham, *Six Existentialist Thinkers*. Routledge & Kegan Paul, London, 1961, p. 98.
5. Heidegger reserves the expression "world" as a term for its third signification. While using it in its first signification he marks it with single quotation. The derivative form "worldy" applies to a kind of Being which belongs to entities which are present-at-hand in the world.
6. H.J. Blackham, p. 100.
7. Johnson J. Puthenpurackal, *Heidegger through Authentic Totality to Total Authenticity*—A unitary approach to his thought in its two phases. Louvain Philosophical Studies-2, Loeuven University Press, 1987, p. 16.
8. *Ibid.*
9. *Ibid.*, p. 17.
10. *Ibid.*, pp. 15-16.
11. *Ibid.*, p. 23.
12. *Ibid.*, p. 24.
13. Johnson J. Puthenpurackhal, p. 22.
14. J. Sallis, *The Concept of the World: A Study in Phenomenological Ontology of Martin Heidegger*. University Microfilms International, Michigan, 1977, p. 90.
15. *Ibid.*, pp. 92-93.
16. Johson J. Puthenpurackal, pp. 18-19.
17. *Ibid.*, p. 20.
18. *Ibid.*, p. 21.
19. *Ibid.*
20. *Ibid.*, p. 35.
21. *Ibid.*, p. 36.

Chapter IV

Dasein, Care and Death

In the preceding chapter we have elucidated Being-in-the-world as the primordial structural whole of Dasein. We have analysed its constitutive items, namely, the world, the entity "who," is in the world and Being-in as such. In the process we have dealt with Dasein's Being-there. We have explained the ontological constitution of the disclosedness belonging to Dasein. We have analyzed Dasein's disclosedness as being constituted by state-of-mind, understanding, and disclosure. We have shown it as being characterized by idle talk, curiosity, and ambiguity. We have also shown these characteristics as contributing to the movement of falling which has temptation, tranquillizing, alienation and entanglement as its essential characteristics. Thus we have laid bare the principal features of the entire existential constitution of Dasein. Our task in this chapter is to present a comprehensive interpretation of Dasein's Being as Care and as Being towards death.

In dealing with Dasein's Being as Care Heidegger aims at defining Dasein's structural whole, namely, Being-in-the-world in an existential-ontological manner. He says that the constitution of the Being-in-the-world is so manifold that it obstructs our unified view of it. So, there is a need to look at this structural whole as such phenomenoligically and in a way which is unified. This is possible only by defining the totality of the structural whole in an existential ontological way. It is not enough to define Dasein's average everydayness as "Being-in-the-world which is falling and disclosed, thrown and projecting, and for which its ownmost potentiality-for-Being is an issue, both in its Being alongside the 'world' and in its Being-with others."[1] The structural whole of Being-in-the-world is based upon the Being of Dasein. It becomes clearer only when the structural whole of the Being of Dasein in its everydayness is accessed. And the Being of Dasein in its totality becomes accessible when we look through this whole to a single unitary phenomenon which is already there in this whole. The phenomenon is there in the whole in such a way that it provides the ontological foundation for each item of its structural possibility. The phenomenon is one of the most far-reaching and primordial possibilities of the disclosure of Dasein's Being. Its disclosure is such that in it Dasein brings itself before itself and becomes accessible as simplified in a certain manner. And this phenomenon is none other than *anxiety*[2] which lies in Dasein itself. Anxiety is a basic state-of-mind. It is one of Dasein's possibilities of Being. Anxiety and Dasein as disclosed in it provide the phenomenal basis for grasping Dasein's Being in its primordial totality. The phenomenon of anxiety discloses Dasein as a Being of Care. "Dasein's Being reveals itself as *Care*" (*BT* 227), says Heidegger. There is thus a need to interpret Dasein existentially as Care. We have to demonstrate the fact that Dasein, in expressing anything about itself to itself, interprets itself as Care. Care is a basic existential phenomenon. It has to be distinguished from the phenomena such as will, wish, addiction and urge. These phenomena might be identified with Care. But Care cannot be derived from them. In fact, they are founded upon Care. Since Care is based on anxiety we have to first analyse anxiety as a distinctive way in which Dasein is disclosed.

A. Anxiety as a Distinctive way in Which Dasein is Disclosed

As mentioned above, anxiety is a distinctive state-of-mind in which Dasein gets brought before itself through its own Being. But it is in the face of Being-in-the-world that Dasein has anxiety (*das Wovor der Angst*). Being-in-the-world is that in face of which Dasein is anxious. At the same time Being-anxious discloses the world as world. The world as world is disclosed first and foremost by anxiety. It is disclosed as a mode of state-of-mind. This does not mean that in anxiety the worldhood of the world gets conceptualized. Anxiety is not only a state of mind but it is also anxiety about something. That which anxiety is profoundly anxious (*sich abangstet*) about is not a *definite* kind of Being for Dasein. It is not even a *definite* possibility for it. That which anxiety is anxious about is Being-in-the-world itself. In anxiety what is environmentally ready-to-hand sinks away. So also the entities within-the-world do sink away. Anxiety thus takes away the possibility of understanding itself. It throws Dasein back upon that which it is anxious about. That is, anxiety throws Dasein back upon its authentic potentiality-for-Being-in-the-world. It individualizes Dasein as something that understands, projects itself essentially upon possibilities. Thus anxiety, with what it is anxious about, discloses Dasein as Being-possible. It discloses Dasein "as the only kind of thing which it can be of its own accord as something individualized in individualization (*Vereinzeltes in der Vereinzelung*)" (*BT* 232).

Anxiety enables Dasein to manifest itself in its Being towards its ownmost potentiality-for-Being. That is, in anxiety, Dasein manifests itself as Being-free for the freedom of choosing itself. It enables Dasein to take hold of itself. It brings Dasein face to face with its Being-free for the authenticity of its Being. Anxiety individualizes Dasein and discloses it as solipsistic. That is, anxiety brings Dasein face to face with its world. It brings face to face with itself as Being-in-the-world. This is what is meant by solipsism in its existential sense. At the same time, in anxiety one feels 'uncanny' or 'unhomelike.' In it Dasein finds itself in a peculiar kind of indefiniteness. Dasein experiences the feeling of being 'nothing, nowhere and not-being-at-home (*das Nichtzuhause-sein*). The feeling of uncanniness, nothing and nowhere brings Dasein back from its state of falling in which Dasein is absorbed in the world. Anxiety puts an end to Dasein's sense of everyday familiarity. It makes Dasein individualized as Being-in-the-world. It endows Dasein with the existential meaning of Being-in as against the categorical signification of insideness. It is with anxiety that "Being-in enters into the existential mode of the not-at-home" (*BT* 232).

Dasein's uncanniness is a threat to Dasein's everyday lostness in the 'they.' It comes from Dasein itself and reaches Dasein itself. It belongs to Dasein's essential state of Being-in-the-world. It exists in the mode of a state-of-mind and never as being present-at-hand. As a phenomenon that is existential, uncanniness exists always in a mode of factical Being-there. From an existential-ontological point of view, the uncanniness or the not-at-home is a primordial phenomenon. Heidegger says that since anxiety is always hidden in the Being-in-the-world, the latter is ever of the nature of fear. He also says that fear is nothing but anxiety which is hidden from itself. Real anxiety becomes rare when pubicness and falling are dominant. It is rare because Dasein for the most part remains concealed from itself. In fact, anxiety discloses Dasein's Being-in-the-world in a distinctive way, since it individualizes Dasein. Individualization brings Dasein back from its falling. It reveals to Dasein that authenticity and inauthenticity are its basic possibilities which show themselves in anxiety as they are in themselves and undisguised by the entities within-the-world, to which, proximally and for the most part, Dasein clings. "Finally anxiety reveals Dasein in its referential dependence on the world (*Sein-bie-der-Welt*)"[3].

B. Dasein's Being as Care: An Existential-Ontological Interpretation

As it has already been mentioned, Dasein is an entity for which, in its being, that Being is an issue. Dasein is also a self-projective Being towards its ownmost potentiality-for-Being. It is a Being which has already compared itself with a possibility of itself. This shows that Dasein is a Being which is already ahead of itself. It is always beyond itself. (*Uber sich hinaus*). The structure of Being-ahead-of-itself pertains to the whole of Dasein's constitution. It characterizes Dasein's Being-in-the-world. So "Being-ahead-of-itself" does not signify Dasein's tendency of being isolated in a worldless subject. On the contrary, it signifies Dasein's being "ahead-of-itself-in-already-being-in-a-world" (*BT* 236). And Heidegger holds that the formally existential totality of Dasein's ontological structural whole must be grasped in the structure, namely, ahead-of-itself-Being-already-in-the-world as Being-alongside entities encountered within-the-world. Heidegger holds that this structure must be grasped essentially as a unitary phenomenon. He also maintains that this phenomenon is the very Being of Dasein and it fills in the meaning of the term "Care" (*Sorge*) (*BT* 237).

Being-in-the-world is essentially Care. So Care does not stand for an isolated attitude of the "I" towards itself. It also cannot stand for some special attitude towards the self. The expression 'Care for oneself' ("Selbst-sorge") is a tautology since Care is inherent to "Being-ahead-itself which is characterized by the Being-already-in-the-world alongside the entities within-the-world. So Care is a primordial structural totality of Dasein. It lies a priori 'before' (*Vor*) every factical attitude and the situation of Dasein. Every activity of Dasein has the character of Care. Even the simple act of ascertaining something present-at-hand has the character of Care. Even the acts like resting and enjoying exhibit it. Care is more primordial than the phenomena of willing and wishing, urge and addiction. Willing and wishing are posterior to Care. They are rooted in Dasein as Care. Same is the case with urge and addiction. They too are grounded in Dasein as Care. Heidegger says, "The phenomenon of Care in its totality is essentially something that cannot be torn asunder; so any attempt to trace it back to special acts or drives like willing and wishing or urge and addiction, or to construct it out of these, will be unsuccessful" (*BT* 238).

Heidegger says that we must exhibit a still more primordial phenomenon which provides an ontological support for the unity and the totality of the structural manifoldness of Care. He holds that in explicating Dasein's Being as Care, he is only conceptualizing existentially what has already been disclosed in an ontico-existentiell manner. What is ontologically new in the interpretation of Dasein's Being as Care is ontically quite old. He contends that the existential interpretation of Dasein as Care is not a mere fabrication but well-grounded in the ancient interpretation of man. To show this Heidegger cites a document which is pre-ontological in character. The document comprises a fable in which Dasein's interpretation of itself as Care is embedded. The fable is as follows:

> Once when 'Care' was crossing a river, she saw some clay; she thoughtfully took a piece and began to shape it. While she was meditating on what she had made, Jupiter came by. 'Care' asked him to give it spirit, and this he gladly granted. But when she wanted her name to be bestowed upon it, he forbade this, and demanded that it be given his name instead. While 'Care' and Jupiter were disputing, Earth arose and desired her own name be conferred on the creature, since she had furnished it with part of her body. They asked Saturn to be their arbiter, and he made the following decision, which seemed a just one: "Since you, Jupiter, have given it spirit, you shall receive that spirit at its death; and since you, Earth, have given its body, you shall receive its body. But since 'Care' first shaped this creature, she shall possess it as long as it lives. And because there is now a dispute among you as to its name, let it be called *homo*, for it is made out of *humus* (earth)" (*BT* 242).

Heidegger points out that the fable mentioned above is very significant, since it reveals the fact that the ontological interpretation of Dasein as Care has already been sketched out in elemental ways. The fable reveals that the human Dasein belongs to 'Care' for its time. It also shows that 'Care' is prior to man's body (earth) and spirit. It is in Care that Dasein has the source of its Being. Dasein is dominated through and through by Care. It is held fast by Care as long as it is in the world. Being-in-the-world has the stamp of 'Care' which accords with its Being. The fable also tells the truth that the decision regarding the primordial Being of the creature shaped by 'Care' is left to Saturn who symbolizes Time. That is, the fable characterizes man's essence by the kind of Being which dominates his temporal sojourn in the world. And it is not in consideration of its Being that the creature gets it name "*homo*." It is only in relation to what it consists, namely, *humus* that the creature gets its name. Heidegger contends that the phenomenon of Care discloses several structures of Dasein, since Care determines what is basically specific to Dasein. It is by Care that man can accomplish his perfection. In Being-free for his ownmost possibilities, man can transform himself into what he can be. This can be accomplished by 'Care' only (*BT* 243).

Besides the fable, the ancient thinkers like Burdach and Seneca have referred to the phenomenon of Care. Burdach uses the term "Care" in its two senses. Firstly, the term "Care" means anxious exertion and secondly, it means 'Carefulness' and 'devotedness.' Seneca says that the good of God is fulfilled by his Nature, whereas the good of man is fulfilled by *Care* (*Cura*). Heidegger holds that the meanings of Care as we find in the fable, in Burdach and Seneca are only ontical in nature. Their interpretation of Care is pre-ontological generalization and theoretical in character. They only say that all our ways of behaving are full of Care and guided by our devotedness to something or the other. But the existential-ontological interpretation of Care treats it as Dasein's state of Being which is already underlying in every case. It conceives Care as primordial condition for the possibility of the cares of life and devotedness. Heidegger therefore holds that we have to move forward from Dasein's pre-ontological interpretation of itself to the existential conception of Dasein as Care. The analytic of Dasein should change its direction from the questionable traditional accounts of Care and man. It is only by considering Care in its existential-ontological sense that we can arrive at the right foundation of the analytic of Dasein. It is only then that the question, namely, the meaning of Being in general can be appropriately answered.

C. Care and Reality

Heidegger says that ontologically, the term "Reality" stands for the Being-of-the-entities present-at-hand within-the-world (*res*). It signifies that entities within-the-world are ontologically conceivable only if the phenomenon of within-the-world-ness has been clarified. And the phenomenon of within-the-worldness is based upon the phenomenon of the *world* which is an essential item in the structure of Being-in-the-world. Being-in-the-world, in turn, is bound up ontologically in the structural totality of Dasein's Being. And Care is precisely this structural totality of Dasein's Being. Proper analysis of Reality is possible on the foundations of this totality. The character of Reality becomes ontologically intelligible only when the entities within-the-world are conceived as belonging to the basic constitution of Dasein, the Being of which is Care. Heidegger maintains that "Reality," which is essentially related to entities within-the-world, has readiness-to-hand and presence-at-hand as its modes. Reality has no priority among the modes of the Being of entities within-the-world. Reality is a kind of Being which cannot even characterize either the world or Dasein in an ontologically appropriate manner. Dasein and the world have such a kind of Being that they cannot be conceived in terms of Reality and substantiality. Therefore, Reality has to be conceived in terms of Being-in-the-world and Dasein's being as Care. Reality is intelligible when it "is referred back to the phenomenon of Care" (*BT* 255). And since Care is the Being of Dasein, Reality is ontologically grounded in the Being of Dasein. But the fact that Reality is ontologically grounded in the Being of Dasein does not mean that Reality exists only as long as Dasein exists. It only means there is an understanding of Being as long as there is Dasein. It is Being and not the entities that is dependent upon understanding. That is to say, it is Reality and not the Real that is dependent upon Care.

D. Dasein, Disclosedness, and Truth

Heidegger is of the view that the problem of truth certainly falls within the range of the problematic of fundamental ontology, since truth has a primordial connection with the question of Being. He holds that the essence of truth is necessarily related to the kind of Being which truth possesses. Investigation into what is truth involves clarification of the ontological meaning of the kind of talk centred round the assertion that 'there is truth.' Accordingly Heidegger begins his inquiry into the phenomenon of truth with the traditional conception that truth is the agreement of knowledge with its object. But he contends that the characterization of truth as 'agreement' is very general and empty. He holds that agreement presupposes relationship. The agreement of something with something has the formal character of a *relation* of something to something. Every truth, and therefore knowledge as well, is a relation, since, according to general opinion, what is true is also knowledge. The truth or knowledge has the relational character of the 'just as.' So there is a need to inquire into the foundations of this relationship of agreement between the subject and object. The phenomenon of truth becomes evident only when the ontological meaning of the relation between the ideal and the real is explicated. Heidegger characterizes this relation as *subsisting* (*Bestand*) (*BT* 259).

Heidegger is of view that the phenomenon of truth is disclosed only when the Being that belongs to knowledge is reached. Truth comes into Being when knowing demonstrates itself *as true*. Truth becomes phenomenally explicit in knowledge itself. It is by demonstrating itself as knowledge that knowledge is assured of its truth. It is in the context of demonstration that the relation of agreement as subsistence becomes vivid. For instance, someone with his back turned to the wall makes the *true assertion* that 'the picture on the wall is hanging askew.' This assertion *demonstrates* itself when the man who makes it, turns round and *perceives* the picture hanging askew on the wall. Here, the assertion is a way of Being towards the picture about which assertion is made. The perceiving demonstrates that this picture *is* the very entity which one has in mind when making the assertion. Here the truth that the picture is pointed out by the Being in which the assertion is made, gets confirmation. And what gets demonstrated in the demonstration of turning around and perceiving the picture is the Being-uncovering of the assertion. In this demonstration the knowing remains to be related solely to the entity itself. It is through this entity that the confirmation gets enacted. That is, the entity which one has in mind shows itself *just* as it is in itself. It shows that it is just as it gets pointed out in the assertion. It shows that it gets uncovered as being in its self-sameness (*BT* 261).

Heidegger maintains that in the matters of truth or knowledge what is to be demonstrated is not an agreement of knowing with its object; it is not even an agreement of the psychical with the physical; nor is it an agreement between contents of consciousness. In *Being and Time,* Heidegger gives a rather lengthy analysis of the 'correspondence' theory of truth only to show finally that "it is empty and inadequate in itself."[4] In fact, it is solely the Being-uncoveredness (*Entdeckt-sein*) of the entity itself that is to be demonstrated by the assertion. In other words, what is to be demonstrated is *that entity* in the "how" of its uncoveredness.[5] This uncoveredness is confirmed when the entity which is put forward in the assertion shows itself as that very same thing. 'Confirmation' signifies the entity's showing itself in its selfsameness. It is the basis of the entity's showing-itself that the confirmation is accomplished. Confirmation is possible only when the knowing itself is a *Being towards* Real entities. It is only as a Being that *uncovers* that knowing asserts and gets confirmed. An assertion *is true* only when it uncovers the entity as it is in itself. A true assertion points out, lets the entity be seen in its uncoveredness. So the truth or the Being-true of an assertion must be understood as Being-uncovering. Being-true as Being-uncovering is possible only on the background of Being-in-the-world which is the basic mode of the Being of Dasein. And it is the structure of Being-in-the-world that is the *foundation* for the primordial phenomenon of truth. "Thus truth has by no means the structure of an agreement between knowing and the object in the sense of a likening of entity (the subject) to another (the object)" (*BT* 261).

E. The Primordial Phenomenon of Truth

Heidegger says that the definition of truth as Being-uncovering is not arbitrary or dubious. It is also not entirely new, a bolt from the blue. It does not plunge the good old tradition into nullity. The definition of truth as Being-uncovering was understood in the ancient philosophy in its pre-phenomenological manner. It contains only the *necessary* interpretation of what was primordially surmised in the *oldest* tradition. Heidegger holds that the idea of taking entities out of their unhiddenness or uncoveredness is there in the ancient concept of *logos*. The phenomenon of truth in the sense of uncoveredness can be found even in the philosophical doctrine of Heraclitus which explicitly deals with the issue of *logos*. According to Heidegger the term "*logos*" tells how entities comport themselves.[16] It expresses the unhiddenness in which Dasein uncovers itself. Thus, in defining truth as uncoveredness, Heidegger has not rejected the tradition altogether but has appropriated it in a primordial manner. The definition of truth as uncoveredness is not a mere explanation of the word "truth." The definition in fact emerges from the analysis of the true ways in which Dasein comports itself. Being-true as Being-uncovering is a way of Being for Dasein. Truth, in its primordial sense is what makes this uncovering possible. "The most primordial phenomenon of truth is first shown by existential-ontological foundations of uncovering" (*BT* 263), says Heidegger.

For Being-in-the-world, uncovering is a way of its Being. Dasein's circumspective concern uncovers entities within-the-world. These entities therefore become that which has been uncovered. The entities thus are true in the second sense. In this sense truth does not mean Being-uncovering but Being-uncovered. And Dasein that is true exists only in its primary sense of Being-uncovering. Dasein comports itself in ways of Being-uncovering. The analysis of the worldhood of the world and the entities thereof has shown that the uncoveredness of the entities is grounded in the world's disclosedness. Disclosedness is also the basic character of Dasein. It is in accordance with its disclosedness that Dasein is its 'there.' Disclosedness is constituted by the items of the world, understanding, and discourse. It pertains equiprimordially to the world, to Being-in, and to the self. Disclosedness is also hidden in the structure of Care in which Dasein is already ahead of itself as Being alongside entities within-the-world. Uncoveredness manifests itself in and through the structure of Care. Thus the phenomenon of truth is attained only with Dasein's disclosedness. Dasein is essentially its disclosedness and it uncovers itself as something disclosed. So it must be said that Dasein is essentially true. We can also make the assertion, "Dasein is '*in the truth.*'" Ontologically the meaning of this assertion is that the disclosedness of Dasein's ownmost Being belongs to its existential constitution. Heidegger explicates the full existential purport of this assertion by considering the four phenomena namely, disclosedness, thrownness, projection and falling. (1) Disclosedness in general essentially belongs to Dasein's state of Being. It encompasses the whole structure of Being which has become explicit through the phenomenon of Care. Care embraces both Being-in-the-world and Being alongside entities within-the world. The uncoveredness of entities is equiprimordial with the Being of Dasein and its disclosedness. (2) Thrownness of Dasein is constitutive of Dasein's disclosedness. In thrownness Dasein is disclosed as Being already in a definite world alongside a definite range of definite entities. (3) Projection of Dasein discloses it as Being towards its potentiality-for-Being. Dasein discloses itself to itself in and as its ownmost potentiality-for-Being. Disclosing in terms of its ownmost potentiality-for-Being is the *authentic* disclosedness of Dasein. It shows the phenomenon of the most primordial truth in the mode of authenticity. The most primordial and *authentic* disclosedness in which Dasein understands and discloses itself as a potentiality for Being is the *Truth of existence*. (4) Falling of Dasein discloses Dasein as Being lost in its world. In falling Dasein's understanding has diverted thither. Being absorbed in the "they," Dasein is dominated by the way things are publicly interpreted. What is disclosed gets disguised and closed off by idle talk, curiosity and ambiguity. Entities have been disguised and Dasein's Being towards them has been uprooted. They show themselves in the mode of semblance and what has already been uncovered gets disguised again. Thus the state of Dasein's Being as falling reduces Dasein to *untruth*: "Because Dasein is essentially falling, its state of Being is such that it is in untruth" (*BT* 264).

Heidegger says that Dasein is already both in the truth and the untruth.[7] The statement that 'Dasein is in the truth' equally states that 'Dasein is in untruth,' as well. In so far as Dasein has been disclosed, it has also been closed off. In so far as entities within-the-world have been uncovered along with Dasein, they have also been covered up or disguised. In its existential-ontological sense the very Being-in-the-world has the character of both truth and untruth. Being-in-untruth is as much an essential characteristic of Being-in-the-world as Being-in-truth is. The state of Dasein's Being as *thrown projection* is the condition for Being-in-the-world as characterized by truth and untruth. And Dasein's state of thrown projection is constitutive of the structure of Care. Heidegger holds that the way of uncovering is achieved in distinguishing between truth and untruth. It consists in *understandingly* making one's decision for truth rather than for untruth. Dasein should explicitly appropriate what has already been uncovered; it should defend what is uncovered against all semblance and disguise. It should thereby assure itself of its uncoveredness again and again (*BT* 265).

F. The Being of Truth and Its Presupposition

As mentioned above, Dasein is essentially in the truth, since disclosedness is its essential characteristic. So also 'there is' truth only in so far as and so long as Dasein is. Entities are uncovered only when Dasein is and as long as Dasein is. For instance, Newton's laws, the principles of contradiction, or truth in any other sense are true only as long as Dasein *is*. "Before there was Dasein, there was no truth, nor will there be any after Dasein is no more. For, in such a case truth as disclosedness, uncovering, and uncoveredness, *cannot* be" (*BT* 269). In this connection, Heidegger contends that it is not possible to adequately prove that there are eternal truths, since the proof of an eternal truth warrants proof that Dasein has been and will be for all eternity. The principle of eternal truth remains to be a fanciful contention as long as the proof of the eternity of Dasein remains to be outstanding. Mere belief in eternal truth does not have any legitimacy. This shows that all Truth is relative to Dasein's Being. Since truth is the essential character of Dasein, truth is meaningless in the absence of Dasein. This does not mean that truth is subjective in the sense that truth is dependent on the subject's discretion. Since truth is uncovering which is most its own, asserting is taken out of the province of subjective discretion and Dasein is brought face to face with the entities themselves. Truth can be taken out of Dasein's discretion precisely because truth as uncovering is a kind of Being which belongs to Dasein. Even the truth in the sense of 'universal validity' is rooted in the fact that Dasein can uncover entities in themselves. Thus truth in its proper sense is ontically possible only in the 'subject,' namely, the Being of Dasein. The existential conception of truth stands or falls with the Being of the subject, called, Dasein (*BT* 270).

Heidegger further maintains that we presuppose that 'there is truth' because 'we' *are* in the truth. Truth is the kind of Being which Dasein possesses. We do not presuppose truth as something 'outside' us and 'above' us. We do not presuppose it as we do the other 'values.' In fact, it is not 'we' who presuppose truth; but it is truth what first makes presupposing possible. Truth makes it possible for us to *be* such that we presuppose anything at all. To presuppose is to understand something as the ground for the Being of some other entity. This kind of understanding of an entity is possible only on the ground of disclosedness which is the Being of Dasein. To presuppose truth therefore means to understand truth as something for the sake of which Dasein is. But as the Being of Care, Dasein is already ahead of itself in each case. And presupposing lies in Dasein's state of Being as Care which is already ahead of itself. Neither the presupposing nor the truth belongs to the entities other than Dasein. They solely belong to Dasein only: "We must 'make' the presupposition of truth because it *is* one that has been 'made' already with the Being of the 'we'" (*BT* 271).

Heidegger is of the view that the existence of Dasein as well as truth is necessary. He declares that Dasein *must be* and it *must be* in the same way as the truth *must be*, since the truth is nothing but Dasein's disclosedness. The necessity of the existence of the both belongs to Dasein's essential thrownness into the world.

Dasein has never decided freely whether it wants to come into itself or not. And it will never be able to take such a decision. It is quite incomprehensible why *truth* and Dasein *must be*. Scepticism cannot refute the existence of Dasein and truth. In denying them scepticism stops half way. As a formal argument scepticism shows that if anything gets judged, truth has been presupposed. This suggests that 'truth' belongs to an assertion. In other words, this also suggests that pointing out is an uncovering. But when the sceptic says this, he or she "*has to clarify why* that in which there lies the ontological ground for this necessary connection between assertion and truth as regards their Being, must be as it is" (*BT* 271). That is, the sceptic can not explain the nature of the necessary connection between assertion and truth. So also the kind of Being which belongs to truth is left completely obscure. Likewise, the meaning of presupposing and the meaning of the ontological foundation of presupposing in Dasein are left unclarified. Moreover, we have to recognize the fact that even when nobody *judges*, truth already gets presupposed in the very existence of Dasein. Heidegger further says that just as the Being of truth can never be proved, a sceptic can never be refuted. There is also no need to refute a sceptic who denies truth. It is not possible that there exists an 'actual sceptic.' It is not possible that a sceptic who denies truth factically *is*. The existence of such a sceptic is impossible since it implies obliteration of both Dasein and truth. Heidegger says, "In so far he *is*, and has understood himself in this Being, he has obliterated Dasein in the desperation of suicide; and in doing so, he has also obliterated truth. Because Dasein, for its own part, cannot first be subjected to proof, the necessity of truth cannot be proved either. It has no more been demonstrated that there ever has 'been' an 'actual' sceptic (though this is what has at bottom been believed in the reputations of scepticism, in spite of what these undertake to do)' than it has been demonstrated that there are any 'eternal truths.' But perhaps such sceptics have been more frequent than one would innocently like to have when one tries to bowl over 'scepticism' by formal dialectics" (*BT* 271-72).

Thus by analyzing the phenomenon of Care in its various structures, Heidegger has clarified the state of Dasein's Being to which an understanding of Being belongs. The explication of Care as Dasein's Being has brought out the clear distinction between the Being of Dasein and the modes of Being which characterize entities other than Dasein. In this process the phenomena of understanding, reality and truth have been elucidated. At the same time, the transparent method of interpreting Being by understanding it has also been made clear. The analytic of Care has revealed the primordial state of Dasein's Being. But the analytic of Care is not sufficient to define the meaning of Being in general. The phenomenon of Care has not been able to disclose the most primordial existential-ontological state of Dasein. The manifold structures of Care have not revealed the most primordial totality of the Being of the factual Dasein. Investigation into Care has not exposed Dasein as a whole.

G. Ontological Interpretation and Hermeneutical Situation

The analysis of Dasein carried out so far is only preparatory. The analysis has revealed to us that the essential structures of Being-in-the-world are centred round in disclosedness. We found the basic state of Dasein in Being-in-the-world. The totality of Being-in-the-world as a structural whole has shown itself to be as Care in which the Being of Dasein is included. The analyses have shown existence as the essence of Dasein. Existence indicates that Dasein is a potentiality for Being which makes an issue of that Being itself. In every case, I myself am the entity which is an issue for itself. The analysis of the phenomenon of Care has given us an insight into concrete constitution of existence. That is, it has revealed to us the primordial connection of Care with Dasein's facticity and its falling.

But what we are seeking through the analytic of Dasein is to work out the answer to the basic question of all ontology, namely, the question about the meaning of Being in general. We have to lay bare the horizon within which the Being in general becomes intelligible. This requires clarifying the possibility of having an understanding of Being. That is, we have to clarify the possibility of an understanding which belongs to the constitution of Dasein. We have to *radically* clarify that the understanding of Being is an essential element in Dasein's Being. We have to interpret Dasein primordially in itself with regards to its Being. Interpreting Dasein ontologically *qua* Care is not a primordial interpretation of it. We have to first find out the criteria which can assess whether the existential analytic of Dasein is primordial or not. This warrants the question—what is meant by the *primordiality* of an ontological interpretation?

Ontological interpretation is a working-out and an appropriation of an understanding. It has its own presuppositions such as fore-having, fore-sight and fore-conception. Heidegger calls the totality of them the *hermeneutical situation* (*BT* 275). In it an entity is to be laid bare with regards to its own state of Being. It demands us to give a phenomenal characterization of the entity we have taken as our theme. We have to bring the entity into the scope of our fore-having with which all the subsequent steps of our analysis must confirm. These steps are to be guided by whatever fore-sight is possible as to the kind of Being which the entity may possess. Our fore-having and fore-sight will then give us a sketch of a particular way of conceiving the entity. And all the structures of Being have to be raised to the level of conceiving.

Ontological Interpretation becomes a *primordial* one when its *hermeneutical situation* is made secure in conformity with the phenomena. The entity which it has taken as its theme should as a *whole* be brought into the fore-having. We have to go beyond a first sketch of the Being of this entity. We have to grasp the Being of this entity as a whole and in the unity of all its structural items which are actual as well as possible. Then only we can have a fore-sight of the Being of the entity. The fore-sight enables us to formulate and answer the question of the meaning of Being as a whole. Even the fore-having of the ontological Interpretation of Care as the totality of the structural whole of Dasein's constitution has not brought Dasein into view as a whole. It has not brought the whole of Dasein in its everydayness, from its birth to death, into phenomenological view. So the ontological interpretation should take up the task of putting Dasein as a whole into its fore-having. It means that the ontology should raise the question of Dasein's potentiality-for-Being-as-a-whole. The Being of Dasein is such that there is always something outstanding to it; the something outstanding is that which Dasein can be and will be. And it is the 'end' that belongs to the something that is outstanding. The end of Dasein's Being-in-the-world is death. Death belongs to existence as a potentiality-for-Being. It limits and determines in every case whatever is possible for Dasein. Death is not to be treated as a mere character of Dasein; death as the character of Dasein shows Dasein only in an existentiell *Being towards death* (*Sein Zum Tode*). Death has to be treated as an existential structure of Dasein, for "it proves to be the ontologically constitutive state of Dasein's potentiality-for-Being-a-whole" (*BT* 277). The ontological interpretation therefore must obtain an adequate conception of death. It means, it must obtain death in its ontological and existential sense. Only then can the whole of existing Dasein be brought into existential fore-having.

H. Dasein as a Whole and the Death of Others

As it has been mentioned above, Dasein acquires its wholeness in death. In death, Dasein loses the Being of its 'there' and is no-longer-itself. In death, Dasein cannot experience its transition of not-being-itself. The possibility of experiencing death as something experienced is denied to Dasein. The impossibility of experiencing and understanding its own death makes the death of Others very significant. The death of Others enables Dasein to have an Objective access to its own termination (*Beendigung).* That is, it is through the death of Others that "Dasein's death becomes 'Objectively' accessible" (*BT* 281). Since Dasein is essentially Being-with-Others, it can experience death Objectively. The fact that death is Objectively given in Dasein's relation to Others, enables us to have an ontological delimitation of Dasein's totality.

Like Dasein itself, even the Dasein of Others is no-longer-Dasein when it meets its death. In death, the Dasein of Others is no more in the sense of Being-no-longer-in-the-world; it means losing one's Being-in-the-world. But the paradox is that when someone has died, his Being-no-longer-in-the-world is still a Being. This Being is no more a Being of a corporeal Thing which we encounter, but yet it is a kind of Being-just-present-at-hand-and-no-more. In dying of the Other we can experience the remarkable phenomenon of Being which is the change-over of an entity from Dasein's kind of Being (or life) to no-longer-Dasein. The death or the *end* of a Dasein is its *beginning* as something present-at-hand. Even the corpse is something more than a mere corporeal Thing. The corpse which is present-at-hand is still a possible object for the student of anatomy. It is something which is just-present-at-hand-and-no-more. It is more than a *lifeless* material thing. In it we encounter something *unalive*, which has lost its life. The anatomy student's understanding of the corpse is oriented to the idea of life. Heidegger distinguishes the 'deceased' (*Der Verstorbene*) from the dead person (*dem Gestorbenen*). The deceased has been torn away from those who have remained behind (*den Hinterbliebenen*). The deceased is an object of concern in the ways of funeral rites, internment, and the cult of graves. In his kind of Being, the deceased is 'still more' than just an item of equipment and environmentally ready-to-hand. Those who have remained behind him are still with him. They are alongside him in their mourning and commemoration. They are with him in a mode of respectful solicitude. Whereas the relationship which one has towards the dead is not a *concernful* Being-alongside something ready-to-hand. In the Being-with the dead (*dem Toten*), the deceased *himself* is more factically there. But Being-with implies Being with one another in the same world: "The deceased has abandoned our 'world' and left it behind. But in terms of that world (*Aus ihr her*) those who remain can *still be with him*" (*BT* 282).

So we have to take the no-longer-Dasein of the deceased with greater phenomenal appropriateness. This is the proper way of Being-with the dead. This will reveal the fact that in the death of the Other, what in fact we do *not* experience is the authentic Being-come-to-an-end of the deceased. Although death reveals itself as a loss, its loss is such as is experienced by those who remain. The dying of Others is not something which we experience in a genuine sense. We have no way of access to the loss-of-Being which the dying man 'suffers': we cannot experience the dying man's suffering as such. At most we are always just there alongside it. It may be possible for us to experience ourselves 'psychologically' the dying of Others. But we can never grasp the way-to-be with the coming-to-an-end of the Other. However, Heidegger is concerned with the ontological meaning of the dying of the person who dies. He is concerned with a possibility of Being which belongs to the dying person. This concern is not with the psychological way of grasping the dying of the Other.

Heidegger regards the dying of Others as a substitute theme for the ontological analysis of Dasein's totality. This idea is based on the presupposition that any Dasein may be substituted for another at random. It means that one Dasein *can be represented* by another Dasein. And what cannot be experienced in one's own Dasein is accessible in that of a stranger. The fact of

Dasein's representability "belongs to its possibilities of Being-in and Being-with-one another in the world" (*BT* 283). Representability is constantly made use of in manifold ways in our everyday concern. We can always be represented by someone within the range of the 'environment' with which we are mostly concerned. Representation of the one by another extends to the more refined modes of publicly being with one another. It is also germane to the possibilities of concern which are restricted within definite ranges. It also depends upon the possibilities relating to one's age, occupation and social status. Representation is always in relation of oneself with something. That is, representation is meaningful in one's concern with something. Dasein also understands itself in terms of that *with which* it is customarily concerned. That is, Dasein is what it does. Dasein exists in the manner of Being in which we join with one another in absorption in the world of our concern. In this sense the representability is also constitutive of our being with one another: "Here one Dasein can and must, within certain limits, '*be*' another Dasein" (*BT* 284).

The possibility of representing breaks down when it comes to the question of representing the possibility-of-Being of Dasein's death as such. That is, representing cannot work in the case of Dasein's coming to an end which gives it its wholeness. It means no one can take Other's dying away from him. Of course one can die for the sake of another. One can sacrifice oneself for the Other in some definite affair. "Dying for" another does not signify that the Other has his death taken away. Dying is something that every Dasein itself must take upon itself at the time. By its very essence, death is in every case mine. Death signifies a peculiar possibility-of-Being in which the very Being of one's own Dasein is an issue. In dying, mineness and existence are ontologically constitutive for death. Dying is not an event but an existential phenomenon; it has to be understood ontologically and in a distinctive sense. We have to delimit its understanding still more closely. We have to form a purely existential conception of death. We have to interpret death by dispensing with the structures and substructures of entities which are presence-at-hand. We have to analyse death by taking the structures of the phenomena such as "end" and "totality."

The "end" and "totality" are the ways in which Dasein gets a definite character ontologically. They alone can lead us to a primordial interpretation of Dasein. They constitute the wholeness of the Being of Dasein. Ending does not necessarily mean fulfilling oneself. Firstly, ending signifies "stopping." Here "stopping" signifies a sense which is ontologically different. For instance, the statement like 'The rain stops' signifies that rain is no longer present-at-hand. And in the assertion like 'The road stops,' the ending does not make the road disappear. But it is determinative for the road as the one which is present-at-hand. So ending in the sense of stopping signifies either passing over into non-presence-at-hand or Being-present-at-hand only when the end comes. The ending in the sense of the latter may determine two things: it may determine something which is present-at-hand in an *unfinished way*, as a road under construction breaks off; it may also determine the 'finishedness' of something present-at-hand, as the painting which is finished with the last stroke of the brush. But ending in the sense of 'getting finished' does not mean fulfilling. Fulfilling is possible only when something reaches the finishedness that is possible for it. Fulfilling is founded on finishedness. The farmer is a mode of the latter. Heidegger therefore says that none of the modes of ending mentioned above can suitably characterize death as the 'end' of Dasein. Understanding Dasein's dying in the sense of an ending as we have discussed, reduces Dasein to a level of something present-at-hand or ready-to-hand. Heidegger argues that in death or in its ending Dasein does not get itself fulfilled; it has not simply disappeared either; it has not become finished; nor has it become something which is at one's disposal. On the contrary, Dasein, as long as it is, is already its end too: "The *ending* which we have in view when we speak of death," as Heidegger puts it, "does not signify Dasein's Being-at-an-end (*Zu-Ende-sein*), but a Being-towards-the-end (*Sein Zum Ende*) of this entity. Death is a way to be, which Dasein takes over as soon as it is. As soon as man comes to life, he is old enough to die" (*BT* 289).

Heidegger clarifies the phenomenon of Dasein's totality by analyzing the concept of the 'not-yet' which signifies Dasein's constant lack of totality. The "not-yet" belongs to Dasein as long as it exists and it comes to an end with Dasein's end only. It signifies something that is constantly *outstanding* to Dasein. Here the expression "outstanding" means that "which indeed 'belongs' to an entity, but is still missing" (*BT* 286). The outstanding is grounded both upon a belonging-to and a missing. Dasein always exists in the manner that its 'not-yet' or outstanding is not only belonging to it but also missing from it. The 'not-yet' of Dasein is not something which is provisionally and occasionally inaccessible to its experience. The "not-yet" "is" not-yet "actual" at all. The "not-yet" is not something still outstanding in the sense of additive summation. The outstanding of the "not-yet" is not even something which has yet to become accessible. The "not-yet" of the Dasein is such that it is necessary for Dasein that it must *become* or *be* what it is "not-yet." Heidegger tries to define the phenomenon of Dasein's "not-yet" by considering entities to whose kind of Being becoming belongs. He illustrates the problem with an instance of an unriperuit. When a fruit is unripe it goes towards its ripeness. The unripeness is the fruit "not-yet," its outstanding. But the ripening of the fruit is not a piece-meal process. The fruit brings itself to ripeness. The bringing of itself to ripeness is a characteristic of the Being of the fruit. The unripeness of the fruit cannot be eliminated by any external means. The fruit by itself has to come to ripeness of its own accord, since the unripe fruit is its unripeness as it ripens. The "not-yet" of the unripeness is such that it does not refer to anything which stands outside (*aussenstehendes*) the fruit. On the contrary, it refers to the fruit itself in its specific kind of Being. Just as the unripe fruit of the fruit's, which is its "not-yet" is already included in the very Being of the fruit, so also the Being of the "not-yet," which makes up its 'lack-of-totality,' is its constitutive character. Dasein is already its "not-yet," its 'lack of totality' and it is so as long as it is: "That which makes up the lack-of-totality in Dasein, the constant 'ahead-of-itself,' is neither something still outstanding in a summative togetherness, nor something which has not yet become accessible. It is a "not-yet" which any Dasein, as the entity which it is, has to be" (*BT* 288).

I. Existential-Ontological Analysis of Death and Other Interpretations of Death

Heidegger says that the analysis of the phenomena of the ending and the totality of Dasein's Being has shown the phenomenon of death only in a negative way. We have to carry out a positive interpretation of death and its character as an end. This warrants an existential-ontological analysis of death by taking the phenomenon of Care as the clue. As it has already been mentioned, Care is the basic state of Dasein's Being. Death, in its widest sense, is a phenomenon of life which is a Being-in-the world. The existential-ontological character of death can be fixed only by orienting Being-in-the world to Dasein. The existential-ontological essence of death may be defined in terms of life that we find in biology or physiology. But existential-ontological interpretation precedes any biology or physiology of life, since the latter gives only a preliminary conception of life and death. They deal with the life and death of the world of animals and plants. Although Dasein falls into the domain of plants and animals, its death is entirely different from that of them. Plants and animals simply 'perish' whereas Dasein 'dies.' Dasein also dies in the way anything that lives; but its death is distinct in the sense that it is co-determined by its primordial kind of Being. Dasein's dying signifies the way of Being in which Dasein is *towards* its death. Dasein never perishes but can only demise. Thus the existential-ontological interpretation of death precedes the biology or physiology of life. It is also the foundation for any investigation of death, whether it is biographical, historiological, ethnological or psychological. The psychology of dying or death gives information about the 'living' of the person who is 'dying; it does not seek to analyse dying as such; it does not deal with the experiences of the factical demising. Even the interpretation of death among primitive people, and their ways of comporting themselves towards death through magic and cult is based upon the understanding of Dasein. Heidegger says that the metaphysics of death lies outside the preview of the existential-ontological analytic of death. The questions like how and when death comes into the world and what meaning it can have and so on necessarily presuppose an understanding of the character of Being which belongs to Dasein. They also presuppose the ontology of the aggregate of the entities as a whole. Even the issue like what *may be* after death can be raised only by conceiving death in its full ontological-existential sense.

The existential-ontological interpretation of death requires the basic state, namely, Care. We have to define Care as "ahead-of-itself-Being-in-the-world as Being-alongside the entities which we encounter within-the-world" (*BT* 293). This definition has revealed Dasein's fundamental characteristics such as existence (in the ahead-of-itself); facticity (in the Being-already-in); and falling (in the Being-alongside). So death, which belongs to Dasein in a distinctive sense, must be defined in terms of these characteristics. It is only then that we can obtain death as Being-towards-the-end and in its existential-ontological sense.

As an existence, Dasein is not something present-at-hand. So also the death of Dasein is not something not-yet present-at-hand; nor is death something outstanding or impending. But Dasein, as an existence, exists its death as a possibility-of-Being which it has to take over in every case. Death is a possibility of Dasein's Being-in-the-world. With death Dasein stands before itself in its ownmost and non-relational potentiality-for-Being. When it stands before itself in this way, all its relations to Other Daseins have been undone. As a potentiality-for-Being, Dasein cannot outstrip the possibility of death. So death is the possibility of the absolute impossibility of Dasein. "Thus death reveals itself as that possibility which is one's ownmost, which is non-relational and which is not to be outstripped (*uniiberholbare*)" (*BT* 294). The existential possibility of death is based on the fact that Dasein is essentially an existence which is disclosed to itself and ahead-of-itself. The items of disclosure and ahead-of-itself belong to the structures of Care. They derive their primordial significance in Being-towards-death.

Dasein's death as its ownmost and non-relational possibility is the facticity of Dasein. This possibility which can never be outstripped of Dasein is not one which Dasein procures for itself subsequently; it is not the one which Dasein exhibits occasionally in the course of its Being. On the contrary, Dasein has already been *thrown* into this possibility, from the beginning of its existence. Dasein is *thrown* into its death even without any explicit knowledge about it. Dasein is delivered over to its death without any theoretical conception about the fact that death belongs to Being-in-the-world. It is in 'anxiety' that thrownness into death reveals to Dasein in a more primordial way. Anxiety in the face of death is of a different kind. It must not be confused with fear in the face of one's demise. It comes into being in 'the face of that potentiality for-Being which is one's ownmost, non-relational and not to be outstripped. One has anxiety in the face of Being-in-the-world itself. It is simply Dasein's potentiality-for-Being about which one has anxiety. Anxiety is a basic state-of-mind and not a random or an accidental one. Anxiety arises "in the disclosedness of the fact that Dasein exists as thrown Being *towards* its end. Anxiety is thus "the threshold to the self-discovery of Dasein."[8]

Dasein's Being-towards-the-end belongs to Dasein's thrownness. It does not arise through some attitude which appears occasionally. It is a universal characteristic of Dasein. It always reveals itself in a state-of-mind in one way or another. But Dasein proximally and for the most part covers up its ownmost Being-towards-death. It flees in the face of its Being-towards-its-death. Indeed, Dasein is dying as long as it exists, but proximally and for the most part, it does so by way of *falling*.[9] Thus Heidegger makes clear the existential conception of death through the analysis of the items of existence, facticity and falling. As regards its ontological structure, Heidegger seeks to interpret it in terms of Care, since, ontologically, death is grounded in Care. Care is the ontological term for the totality of Dasein's structural whole which includes death. Dasein's Being-towards-death belongs to Dasein's Being itself. It is exhibitable in Dasein's everydayness, even if in a way which is inauthentic. And Care defines Dasein's everydayness. Ontologically speaking, Dasein's Being-in-the-world in its everydayness is Care itself. This is only the preliminary connection between Being-towards-death and Care. For a full ontological sketch of the phenomenon of death, we have to show concrete connection between death and Care. This requires an analysis of Dasein's Being-towards-death in its everydayness.

J. Dasein's Being-towards-Death in its Everydayness

In everydayness we are in the publicness of being with one another. Here death is 'known' as a mishap which is constantly occurring. In everyday publicness, someone or other 'dies' daily and hourly; they may be strangers or neighbours; death is acquainted as a well-known event or as a 'case' in the world. It is encountered in its inconspicuous character. The 'they' has already given away an interpretation for it. It is talked about in a figurative everyday fashion, mostly in an inhibited manner. We talk about death in a manner that it has nothing to do with us. We talk about it in an indefinite way by saying 'one dies.' The phrase "one dies" reveals the kind of an ambivalent Being which belongs to everyday Being-towards-death. It reveals death as that which is proximally not yet present-at-hand for oneself and is therefore no threat. In the phrase "one dies," the "one" is "nobody." The "one" is in no case myself. Thus the phrase levels off death to an occurrence belonging to nobody in particular. "When I say, one dies . . .' I do not mean anybody; that means the one is nobody."[10] This way of talking about death constitutes idle talk. Idle talk about death perverts dying which is essentially mine into an event of public occurrence which 'they' encounter. It treats death as a common event which constantly occurs. It conceals the character of death as a possibility which is non-relational and can never be outstripped. Being utterly ambiguous, idle talk about death puts Dasein in the position of the 'they' which smothers the distinctive potentiality-for-Being which belongs to Dasein's ownmost Self. The 'they' aggravates the temptation to cover up from oneself one's ownmost Being-towards-death. It provides a constant tranquillization about death for one who is dying as well as for those who console him. The 'they' forces Dasein away from its death. It makes itself respectable by regulating the way in which one has to comport oneself towards death. It spreads the opinion among the public that thinking about death is a sign of cowardice and fear. It is a sign of insecurity and a sombre way of fleeing from the world. The 'they' dominates the manner of interpreting things in the public; it decides the state-of-mind which determines our attitude towards death. As it has already been mentioned, Dasein feels anxiety in the face of death; this anxiety brings Dasein face to face with itself; it delivers the fact of death as a possibility which is never to be outstripped. But the 'they' reduces the anxiety 'before' death to fear that arises in the face of an extraneous event which is not faced but passed off as a weakness. Thus the 'they' drives Dasein into an indifferent tranquillity in relation to the 'fact' that one dies, "The cultivation of such a 'superior' and indifferent tranquillity *alienates* Dasein from its ownmost non-relational potentiality-for-Being towards death.[11]

Temptation, tranquillization and alienation constitute the Being of *falling* also. Falling is fleeing in the face of death. It is avoiding the courage of meeting anxiety in the face of everyday Being-towards-death. Falling is the mode of evasion by giving a "new" explanation for death. It is concealing the fact of death by understanding it inauthentically. Actually Dasein is already always dying; it is in the mode of Being-towards-its-death. In falling, Dasein hides this fact from itself by regarding death as just a case of death in Others. Dasein treats death merely as everyday occurrence. It takes death as an event which gives an assurance that 'oneself is still living. However, even in falling and fleeing in the face of death, there is a definite mode of Being-towards-death, though not in an explicit way. Dasein's everydayness and the "they" already have a definite character of death. In these modes, Dasein may not be explicitly engaged in thinking about death. But yet death is constantly an issue for Dasein even in the modes of its Being in everydayness. "Even in average everydayness, this ownmost potentiality-for-Being which is non-relational and not to be outstripped, is constantly an issue for Dasein. This is the case when its concern is merely in the mode of an untroubled indifference towards the uttermost possibility of existence" (*BT* 299).

K. Dasein's Authentic Being-towards-Death

Having analysed the phenomenon of Dasein's everyday Being-towards-death, we have to give a full existential-ontological conception of death. Having examined a preliminary sketch of the existential-ontological conception of death, we have to give a more penetrating interpretation of falling, the Being-towards-death which is an evasion in the face of death. We have analysed *death in the face of which one flees*, in a phenomenally adequate way. We now have to examine phenomenologically the way in which the evasive Dasein itself understands its death.

Falling is an essential tendency of everydayness. In it, Being-towards-death has turned out to be an evasion which conceals the facticality of death. While explaining the process of Dasein's evasion in the face of death, we have moved from a formal sketch of the ontological structure of death to the concrete analysis of everyday Being-towards-the end. In order to secure the full existential conception of death, we have to reverse the direction of our investigation. That is, we have to proceed from the interpretation of everyday Being-towards-the-end.

In explicating everyday Being-towards-death, we have seen how the idle talk of the 'they' regards death as a mere mishap constantly occurring. We have also seen that the idle talk of the 'they' in its everydayness not only conceals the actuality of one's death, but also concedes something like the *certainty* of death. Even in everydayness, nobody doubts that one dies. But the certainty of death realized in everydayness does not imply that kind of Being-certain which corresponds to the way death enters into Dasein. Thus, the certainty is still ambiguous and weak. "By its very meaning, this evasive concealment in the face of death cannot be *authentically* certain of death, and yet it is certain of it" (*BT* 300). The certainty about death in everyday Being-towards-death is only probable and not unconditional. It is only *empirical* and not apodictic. Here the certainty about death is inappropriate in the sense that the certainty is covered up. The uncertainty is inappropriate not in the sense of doubting but in the sense of covering-up of Being-towards-death. In an inappropriate kind of certainty about death, Dasein is not *itself* certain of its death but is under the *illusion* that it is itself certain of its death. Dasein does not try to *think* about death with critical foresight of attaining the highest certainty. Dasein fails to recognize its own Being-towards-death and remains to be indecisive as to the certainty of its death. "So long, however, as Dasein *remains* in the empirical certainty which we have mentioned, death, in the way that it 'is,' is something of which Dasein can by no means become certainty" (*BT* 301).

The everyday-Being-towards-death or the everyday manner in which 'they' talk about death covers up the peculiar characteristic of death's certainty, namely, its indefiniteness. The certainty of death paradoxically lies in its *indefiniteness* of happening at any moment. It is certain that death is possible at any moment; this is the certainty of death in its true sense. Indefiniteness of death goes along with its certainty. But the everyday-Being-towards-death evades the indefiniteness by conferring definiteness upon it. It also covers up death's certainty by covering up its indefiniteness. Thus the talk about death by the 'they' veils death's ownmost character, viz., "a possibility which is certain and at the same time indefinite—that is to say, possible at any moment" (*BT* 302).

Having interpreted the everyday manner in which the 'they' idly talk about death, Heidegger gives the full existential-ontological conception of death. He defines it in the following way: "death, as the end of Dasein, is Dasein's ownmost possibility—non-relational, certain and as such indefinite, not to be outstripped" (*BT* 303). Heidegger claims that this definition of death forms the basis for a Being in which Dasein can be *whole*. Everyday Dasein is already *towards* its end. Dasein in its everydayness is constantly coming to grips with its death. Dasein is towards its death and comes to grips with it but in a fugitive way only. This fact of coming to grips in an inauthentic way shows that death is determinative for Dasein's Being-a-while. Death is not something Dasein ultimately meets in its demise. As a being towards its death, Dasein includes its own "not-yet." The phenomenon of the "not-yet" is derived from the 'ahead-of-itself.' The 'ahead-of-itself' is the structure of Care in general. Care is the basic state of Dasein's Being-in-the-world. So it is Care that makes the Being-a-whole of Dasein possible. Dasein's Being-a-whole becomes truly possible only when Dasein's Care is connected with its death. The kind of Being in which Dasein becomes a whole is possible only when its Being-towards-death is grounded in Care. That is, Dasein's Being-a-whole is founded on its authentic understanding of its Being-towards-death. Our everydayness is a falling evasion in the face of death. It constitutes an inauthentic Being-towards-death. Inauthenticity characterizes a kind of Being into which Dasein has always diverted itself. But inauthenticity is based on the possibility of authenticity. So Dasein need not necessarily and always have to divert itself into inauthenticity. Unlike the entities that are present-at-hand, Dasein is an entity which *exists*. It determines its own character as the kind of entity it is. So Dasein can also understand authentically its own death; it can maintain itself in an authentic Being-towards its-end which is non-relational, certain, indefinite and never to be outstripped. The existential interpretation of death becomes complete when the authentic Being-towards-death is ontologically defined. It is therefore necessary to ontologically interpret the existential conditions of the authentic Being-towards-death (*BT* 304).

As it has been mentioned above, Dasein in its everydayness maintains itself proximally and for the most part in an inauthentic Being-towards-death. And this very inauthentic Being-towards-death forms the basis for the authentic Being-towards-death. Authentic Being-towards-death cannot evade death as its ownmost non-relational possibility. It cannot cover up this possibility by fleeing from it. It cannot also explain it away in accordance with the common sense of the 'they.' The existential projection of an authentic Being-towards-death involves setting forth of the items of this Being. It requires the analysis of these items, since they constitute the understanding of death as a possibility without fleeing and covering it up.

Being-towards-death is a Being towards a possibility, indeed a distinctive possibility of Dasein itself. But death is not something which is ready-to-hand or present-at-hand. Death is a possibility of Dasein's Being but its concernful actualization implies Dasein's actual demise. The demise deprives Dasein of the very ground for existing as Being-towards-death. Thus Being-towards-death does not mean the actualization of death. On the contrary, Being-towards-death indeed means disclosing death understandingly as a possibility without weakening it. It means cultivating Being-towards-death and putting up with it as a possibility without pondering or brooding over death as something impending. It means comporting ourselves towards death in such a way that death reveals itself as a possibility. Heidegger calls this possibility of comporting oneself towards death *anticipation*.

Anticipation is coming closer to death as a possibility. It is coming understandingly closer to death and making its possibility more intense but without making it actual. Anticipation is understanding death without covering it up as a possibility. "It is penetrating into the phenomenon of death as the possibility of the impossibility of any existence at all" (*BT* 307). In anticipation death gives Dasein nothing to be actualized. It gives Dasein nothing which it could itself *be*. Here death is the possibility which reveals the impossibility of Dasein's every way of comporting itself towards anything. It reveals the impossibility of every way of Dasein's very existing. In the anticipation of death in this way, the possibility of death becomes greater. That is, the possibility of death in anticipation discloses itself to be such that it knows no measure at all. It signifies "the possibility of the measureless impossibility of existence" (*BT* 307). Heidegger holds that Being-towards-death is the anticipation of Dasein's potentiality-for-Being, since the very Being of Dasein is anticipation. In its anticipatory potentiality-for-Being, Dasein discloses itself to itself as regards to its death. It projects itself on its own most potentiality-for-Being. It is able to understand itself in the Being that is revealed in its anticipation. This is what is meant by existence in its authentic sense. Anticipation of death thus is the possibility of understanding one's *ownmost* and uttermost potentiality-for-Being. That is, anticipation is the possibility for *authentic existence*. So the authentic existence must be constituted ontologically. This is possible only by setting forth the concrete structure of the anticipation of death. The structure of anticipation has to be delimited phenomenally. The characteristics belonging to this structure must be determined. Only then the anticipatory disclosure becomes the pure understanding of death which is authentic existence. Here understanding does not mean just grasping the verbal meaning but rather understanding oneself in the potentiality-for-Being which reveals itself in projection. It is wrenching oneself away from the idle talk of the 'they.' Thus anticipation allows Dasein to understand the potentiality-for-Being in which its ownmost Being is an issue. This kind of understanding must be taken over by Dasein only. The understanding reveals that death belongs to Dasein in an undifferentiated way; death lays claim to Dasein as an *individual* Dasein. That is, death is utterly non-relational in character. It individualizes Dasein down to itself. This individualization dispenses with all kinds of Being-with-Others and Being-alongside the things. It makes manifest the issue of our ownmost-potentiality-for-Being. Dasein should make its ownmost-potentiality-for-Being-possible of its own accord. Only then can Dasein be itself authentically. Dasein is authentically itself only to the extent that "it projects itself upon its ownmost potentiality-for-Being rather than upon the possibility of the they-self" (*BT* 308).

Anticipation, unlike inauthentic Being-towards-death, does not evade the fact that death is non-relation and not to be outstripped. Instead, anticipation frees itself for accepting the fact that death is not to be outstripped. That is, anticipation works as a way of becoming free for one's own death. It liberates us from our lostness in those possibilities which may accidentally thrust themselves upon us. It enables us to authentically understand and choose the possibility which is not to be outstripped from among the several factical possibilities lying ahead. Anticipation discloses to Dasein that its uttermost possibility lies in giving itself up. It enables Dasein to guard itself against falling behind itself. It shatters our tenaciousness to existence and enables us to face the potentiality-for-Being which we have understood. In anticipation, Dasein dispels the danger of getting outstripped by the possibilities of Others. It overcomes the danger of forcing these possibilities upon itself by interpreting them wrongly. The anticipation of the possibility of death discloses all the possibilities which lie ahead of that possibility. Anticipation thus includes the possibility taking the *whole* of Dasein in advance (*Vorwegnehness) in an existential manner*. In others words, anticipation includes the possibility of Dasein existing as "a whole potentiality-for-Being." (309)

In anticipation, the certainty of death is determined by the kind of truth which *corresponds* to it. It enables Dasein to maintain itself in the truth of the certainty of death. The truth of the certainty of death cannot be computed by ascertaining the cases of death which we encounter. The certainty of death in anticipation is not of the kind that belongs to present-at-hand. It is more primordial than any certainty which relates to entities encountered within-the-world. In anticipation, Dasein can hold death for true; that is, Dasein can understand death as its own; it can fully disclose itself to its own death. Anticipation reveals to Dasein its lostness in the they-self; it brings Dasein face to face with the possibility of being itself in "an impassioned freedom towards death—a freedom which has been released from the illusions of the 'they,' and which is factical, certain of itself and anxious." (311)

NOTES

1. Martin Heidegger, *Being and Time*. Trans. John Macquarie and Edward Robinson, Basil Blackwell, Oxford, 1978, p. 225.
2. "Angst" is the German equivalent of the term "anxiety." It appears as "dread" in the translations of Kierkegaard's works. The terms like "uneasiness" and "malaise" have also been used to signify anxiety.
3. William Richardson, *Heidegger: Through Phenomenology to Thought.* 3rd Edition, Martinus Nijhoff, Hague, 1974, p. 74.
4. Johnson J. Puthenpurackhal, *Heidegger through Authentic Totality to Total Authenticity*—a Unitary Approach to His Thought in its two phases. Louvain Philosophical Studies-2, Leuven University Press, 1987, p. 86.
5. *Ibid.*, p. 87
6. In highlighting the significance of the term *logos* as regards truth, Heidegger says that the ultimate business of Philosophy is to preserve the force of the most elemental words in which Dasein expresses itself. Philosophy has to keep the common understanding from levelling such words off to that unintelligibility which functions in turn as a source of pseudo problems.
7. Here Heidegger reminds us of the Goddess of truth who guided Parmenides and put two paths before him—one of uncovering and another of hiding. This signifies that Dasein was already conceived in terms of truth and untruth in ancient Greek times itself.
8. Thomas Langan, *The Meaning of Heidegger*. Columbia University Press, New York, 1959, p. 28.
9. *Ibid.*, p. 30.
10. Johnson J. Puthenpurackal, p. 43.
11. *Ibid.*, 44.

Chapter V

Dasein, Authenticity and Temporality

In the preceding chapter we have analyzed Dasein in its structural whole as revealing itself as Care. We have shown that the phenomenon of Care determines what is basically specific to Dasein and discloses or uncovers Dasein in truth. We have also interpreted death as the ownmost possibility of Dasein which is certain, non-relational and not-to-be outstripped. The kind of Being in which Dasein becomes a whole is possible only when its Being-towards-death is grounded in Care. We have also examined the conditions required for Dasein's authentic Being-towards-death.

In this chapter we propose to analyse Dasein's potentiality-for-Being which is attested in its existentiell possibility by Dasein itself. The attestation must be such that it must have its source in Dasein's state of Being itself. In this attestation, Dasein must be given to understand itself as something for which authentic existence is possible. The fore-sight of the ontological interpretation so far has revealed the following facts. It has enabled us to define the idea of existence as a potentiality-for-Being. The potential existence is that which understands itself and for which its own Being is an issue to it. The existence is such that it is in each case mine. It is free either for authenticity or for inauthenticity. It is also free for a mode in which authenticity and inauthenticity are undifferentiated. The interpretation, of course, has enabled us to reach a concrete determination of the existentiality of existence. But the determination of existence obtained in the interpretation lacks the essential structure of authenticity. The interpretation has not given us any assurance of having Dasein's existence as a totality. It has only revealed Dasein's essential potentiality-for-Being as 'not-yet' be something which precludes the possibility of grasping Dasein as a whole. Heidegger maintains that the interpretation becomes primordial only when Dasein's essential structure of authentic potentiality-for-Being is brought into the idea of existence. In other words, the interpretation should bring "to light existentially the Being in its possibility of authenticity and totality."[1]

According to Heidegger, the phenomenon of conscience presents Dasein with its authentic potentiality-for-Being. Conscience, like death, demands a genuinely existential interpretation of Dasein. The interpretation founded on conscience gives rise to an insight that "Dasein has an authentic potentiality-for-Being in that it wants to have a conscience (*BT* 279).

As we have already seen, Dasein's lostness in the 'they' has taken it far away from its factical potentiality-for-Being which is closest to it. The 'they' has always kept Dasein from taking hold of the possibilities of its Being, namely, the tasks, the rules, the standards, the urgency and extent of concernful and solicitous Being-in-the-world. The 'they' tacitly 'relieves' Dasein of the burden of explicitly *choosing* these possibilities. Consequently Dasein makes no choices and gets carried along by the nobody. It thus gets itself ensnared in inauthenticity. In order to reverse the process of getting itself ensnared in inauthenticity, Dasein should bring itself back to itself from its lostness in the 'they.' When Dasein thus brings itself back (*Das Sichzuruckholen*) from the 'they,' the they-self gets modified in an existentiell manner and becomes authentic Being-one's-self. The modification gets accomplished by choosing to decide for an authentic potentiality-for-Being. Dasein has to make this decision entirely from its own Self. This authentic potentiality-for-Being should also be attested by the voice of conscience (*Stimme des Gewissens*). Conscience functions as a higher court for Dasein's existence. It is in the conscience that the primordial phenomenon of Dasein lies (*BT* 313). Let us now analyse conscience in a purely existential manner with fundamental ontology as our aim.

A. Conscience as a Call

Existential or ontological analysis of conscience precedes any description of the experiences of conscience. It lies outside of any biological 'explanation' of conscience. The existential interpretation of conscience is different from everyday ontical, common sensical account of it. The ontological analysis of conscience does not mean a theoretical exegesis of conscience. It does not mean the employment of conscience either for proofs of God or for establishing an 'immediate' consciousness of God. As a phenomenon of Dasein, conscience is not a fact which just occurs occasionally but is known as a factuality of Dasein's very Being. It is beyond proofs and counter proofs of the deductive or inductive procedures. Being ontologically different from what is environmentally present-at-hand, conscience *discloses* and gives us 'something' to understand. Conscience as disclosedness of something is a basic state of Dasein which we ourselves are. It is constituted by the phenomena of the state-of-mind, understanding, falling and discourse. A penetrating analysis of conscience reveals it as a *call* (*Ruf*). As a mode of discourse, the call of conscience *appeals* to Dasein to come to its ownmost potentiality-for-Being itself. This is done by way of summoning Dasein to its ownmost Being-guilty. The call of conscience has a corresponding hearing. Our understanding of the appeal or the call unveils itself as our *wanting to have conscience* (*Gewissenhabenwollen*). The wanting to have conscience implies choosing to choose a kind of Being-one's-Self. Heidegger calls this ontological structure, of seeking to choose a kind of Being-one's-Self, *resoluteness*.

As we have already seen, Dasein loses itself in publicness and the idle talk of the 'they.' It fails to *hear* (*Uberhort*) its own

Self and gives itself to listening to the they-self. Dasein should recover from the lostness of failing to hear itself. It must first find itself as something which has failed to hear itself. It must itself be given to a kind of hearing which can interrupt the mode of listening to the they-self. Dasein must appeal to itself, without mediation, to hear itself. It should give a call to itself to break away from *listening away* to the they-self. Here the calling is without any hubbub or the ambiguity of the idle talk. Devoid of curiosity, the calling arouses another kind of hearing which is entirely different from the hearing that is lost in the 'they.' This distinctive kind of calling, which arouses a distinctive hearing and understanding, is called conscience: "That which, by calling in this manner, gives us to understand, is the conscience" (*BT* 316).

The call of conscience is a mode of discourse devoid of vocal utterance. The voice of conscience means giving-to-understand. In it lies a momentum of a push, an abrupt arousal which brings Dasein back to itself. The call of conscience reaches those who want to be brought back to their own Selves. The call is from nowhere, "from afar unto afar" (*BT* 316). Thus conscience as call is a kind of discourse. It is a disclosedness that is constitutive of Dasein's authentic Being. Characterizing conscience in this way gives us a phenomenal horizon for analyzing its existential structure.

The call of conscience is an appeal to Dasein to pay attention to itself. In it, Dasein not only discloses its own world but also discloses and understands itself. The appeal of conscience is a call to one's Self. It is not a call to what Dasein can do; nor is it a call to what Dasein concerns itself in being with one another publicly. The appeal is not at all concerned with the kind of the Being of Dasein which is understood after the manner of the world. It passes over the 'they' and the manner in which Dasein has been publicly interpreted. The call brings the Self back to itself from its hiding place in the 'they.' The Self that gets called in the call of the conscience is not the self, which can become for itself an 'object' on which it can pass judgment; it is not the Self which inertly dissects its 'inner life' with fussy curiosity; nor is it the Self which one has in mind when one gazes analytically at psychical conditions. The Self is not even the one which is turned inwards upon itself and closes itself off from the external world. The Self that the call solely appeals to is none other than Being-in-the-world. Yet the call asserts nothing and gives no information about the events of the world. It has nothing to tell even in the manner of a soliloquy. It dispenses with all kinds of utterance. Call of conscience discourses in the mode of silence. It forces Dasein into the reticence of itself. In calling, 'nothing' gets called to the Self; it is only the Self that gets called or *summoned* (*aufgerufen*) to itself, to its ownmost potentiality-for-Being. The call does not put up the Self for 'trial' but puts forth Dasein into its ownmost possibilities. It summons Dasein to its ownmost potentiality-for-Being-its-Self (*BT* 318).

Although the calling of conscience is not connected with anything like communication, it is not to be regarded as a mysterious voice. The understanding of what is called is not ambiguous or indefinite but clear and unequivocal. The content of the call takes a definite and sure direction. One can easily understand to whom the calling is meant.

B. Conscience as the Call of Care

The above account of the calling of conscience is not an ontologically adequate interpretation of it. We have yet to answer the question—who does the calling? It is not enough to answer—who is called by the calling. We have to establish the relationship between the one who calls and to whom the calling is meant, the appeal is made in the calling. We have to ontologically analyze the relationship in which the two phenomena are interconnected in their Being.

The call of conscience is an appeal to the Self. In the calling the Self has been reached unequivocally and unmistakably. But yet the Self remains to be indefinite and 'empty.' We cannot give a definite answer to the question who or what this self is? The Self to whom the call is meant or appeal is made is without regard for any person. Similarly the caller, who makes the call, is indefinite. The 'caller' maintains itself in conspicuous indefiniteness. The caller does not have a name, a status or origin. We cannot make the caller into something familiar. The caller or that which calls simply holds itself aloof from any way of becoming well-known. Remaining anonymous is its phenomenal character. It does not let itself be drawn into the public-talk and allow itself to be talked about. Yet the peculiar indefiniteness of the caller reveals it in a distinctively positive way. It is a testimony to its total absorption in summoning us to 'something.' It is a testimony to the fact that the caller can be heard in an 'indefinite' way. The identity of the caller remains to be indefinite if we want to listen to it factically in an existentiell way. Yet the facticity of the phenomenon of the calling and hearing can be existentially analysed in definite terms (*BT* 319).

As regards the question—*who* does the calling? Heidegger's answer is that it is Dasein itself. In conscience, Dasein calls itself. In it, Dasein is at the same time both the caller and the one to whom the call is made. Yet the call is an alien power which dominates Dasein. It comes *from* Dasein but yet it is beyond Dasein. This power of the calling can not be explained away biologically. It cannot be taken as a person or God as possessing this power. Heidegger says that there is an ontologically intelligible kind of Being which belongs to both the caller and the calling. He says that the caller is Dasein in its uncanniness; uncanniness is the mysteriousness of the thrownness of Dasein. It determines the state of Dasein's Being-in-the-world. It reveals itself authentically in anxiety and puts Dasein's Being-in-the-world face to face with the 'nothing' of the world. It is in the face this 'nothing' that Dasein is anxious about its ownmost potentiality-for-Being. Heidegger points out that the caller of the conscience is the Dasein which finds itself (*sich befindet*) in the depths of its uncanniness. Dasein in its uncanniness signifies its state of being thrown in the world "as the 'not-at-home'—the bare 'that-it-is' in the 'nothing' of the world" (*BT* 321).

Heidegger says that the caller is unfamiliar to the everyday they-self which is lost in the manifold world of its concern. The caller is the Self which has been individualized down to itself and thrown into the 'nothing' in uncanniness. So the caller is an alien voice to the they-self. The caller in its uncanniness reveals its own potentiality-for-Being in anxiety. The caller is Dasein who is individualized and thrown into the 'nothing.' Out of the depths of uncanniness, Dasein itself, as conscience, calls. And what is called is Dasein itself towards its own potentiality-for-Being. The caller, namely, Dasein calls itself back from the public idle talk of the 'they' into the reticence of his existent potentiality-for-Being. Uncanniness is the ground of both the caller and the called. Uncanniness is the kind of Being in which "Dasein is at the same time both the caller and the one to whom the appeal is made" (*BT* 322). Thus conscience manifests itself as the call of Care. That is, the caller is Dasein which in its thrownness is anxious about its potentiality-for-Being. The one to whom the appeal is made is the very same Dasein, summoned to its ownmost potentiality-for-Being which is Care. Dasein is summoned out of this falling by the appeal of the call. This call is the call of conscience which has its ontological possibility in the fact that Dasein is Care itself. Conscience as the call of Care is also the attestation of Dasein's ownmost possibility. Since conscience as the call of Care is Dasein itself, the attestation lies in Dasein itself (*BT* 324). Heidegger also says that Dasein is guilty in the very heart of its Being. Being-guilty is primordial to Dasein and is prior to its consciousness of guilt. It is more primordial than any knowledge about it. Being-guilty is not the one that arises out of one's failures or omissions; it is not the one which arises through some deed done or left undone. Being-guilty is not a derivative but an essential structure of Dasein. But this primordial Being-guilty remains undisclosed and closed off by Dasein's falling in the 'they.' Heidegger contends that it is only because Dasein is guilty in this way that conscience is possible. The call of conscience reveals the Being-guilty as something which we have to understand. That is, it calls forth to that potentiality-for-Being which in each case I as Dasein am already. it summons Dasein to "*be* 'guilty' authentically, 'guilty' in the way in which it is" (*BT* 333).

Thus hearing the call correctly means understanding oneself in one's ownmost potentiality-for-Being. It means to project oneself upon one's ownmost authentic potentiality for becoming guilty. It means Dasein understandingly letting itself be called forth to its ownmost Being-guilty. It includes Dasein's *becoming free* for the call, its readiness for the potentiality of getting called for. That is, Dasein becomes free to hearing the Call and chooses itself to understand the call: "In understanding the Call, Dasein is in thrall (*horig*) to its ownmost possibility of existence" (*BT* 334). Dasein's choosing itself to hear and understand the call is to choose to have a conscience as Being-free for one's ownmost Being-guilty. Thus understanding the appeal of the call means in fact wanting to have a conscience. Wanting to have a conscience means to be ready to be appealed to. Thus conscience manifests itself as an *attestation* which belongs to Dasein's Being. In this attestation conscience calls Dasein itself face to face with its ownmost potentiality-for-Being. The character of the authentic potentiality-for-Being becomes extentielly concrete when it is thus attested by the call of conscience. The attestation is also accomplished in the very Being of Dasein itself.

C. The Existential Interpretation of Conscience

Heidegger is of the view that although the call of conscience as care does not do anything in terms of positivity, it does not mean that conscience has a negative character. The call may not 'positively' recommend us to do anything. Yet the call has a 'positive' content which we miss "because we expect to be told something currently useful about assured possibilities of taking action which are available and calculable" (*BT* 340). We undermine the essentially 'critical' character of the call, since we interpret it in terms of common-sense concern. The common-sense way of interpreting subsumes conscience under the idea of a business procedure. Common-sense expectations are bound to be disappointed by conscience. Conscience does not give any 'practical' injunctions; it does not even perform reproving or warning type of functions. What the conscience does is that it summons Dasein to existence; its sole function is to call Dasein to its ownmost potentiality-for-Being-its-Self. What the call has in view is *existence* which is ontologically distinct. The phenomenon of *existence* is the 'most positive' of all phenomena. Existence is the ownmost possibility "which Dasein can present to itself, as a calling-back which calls it forth into its factical potentiality-for-being-its-Self at the time" (*BT* 341). This is precisely the existential interpretation of the call of conscience. This is the only right way of understanding it. This is also the authentic way of hearing the call. This is a fully adequate interpretation of what is called in the call. Ordinary interpretations of conscience, its call and the hearing of it arise from the limitations of the way Dasein interprets itself in falling. Ordinary interpretations reveal only what is obvious about conscience. Yet they are by no means accidental but genuine within certain limits, since falling belongs to Care itself. Thus the everyday way of experiencing conscience and ordinary way of interpreting it should be ontologically analyzed and conceptualized for obtaining an existentially primordial account of conscience.

D. Resoluteness and Conscience

As it has already been mentioned, the existential interpretation of conscience exhibits its attestation of Dasein's authentic or ownmost potentiality-for-Being. Let us now examine the existential structure of Dasein's authentic potentiality-for-Being as attested by conscience. As we have already seen, Dasein is a Being of disclosedness. Wanting to have a conscience constitutes the authentic disclosedness of Dasein. This is attested in Dasein itself and by its own conscience. The authentic disclosedness is distinctive in the sense that it constitutes Dasein's reticent self-projection upon its ownmost Being-guilty in which it is ready to face its own anxiety. Heidegger calls this reticent self-projection *resoluteness*. Resoluteness therefore is a distinctive mode of Dasein's authentic disclosedness. Resoluteness is the primordial truth and the authentic Being-of-the Dasein's self. Yet resoluteness is nothing but Dasein's Being-in-the-world only. It does not isolate Dasein from the world and make it a free-floating self-projecting-I. Resoluteness brings the Self into its current concernful Being-along-side what is ready-to-hand. It also brings the Self into solicitous Being with Others. A resolute Dasein lets Others 'be' in their ownmost potentiality-for-Being. It lets co-disclose Others' potentiality in the solicitude which liberates. Being resolute, a Dasein can become the conscience of Others. It is only by authentically Being-their-Selves in resoluteness that people can be together, authentically. Heidegger says that it is only by existing as a resolution that Dasein can disclose itself in resoluteness. Resoluteness is possible only as a resolution (*Entschluss*) which understandingly projects itself. It is in a resolution that the existentiell indefiniteness of resoluteness becomes existentially definite. "Only in a resolution is resoluteness sure of itself" (*BT* 345).

Dasein in its average everyday Being-in-the-world is irresolute (*Unentschlossen*). Irresoluteness is surrendering to the way in which things are interpreted by the 'they.' It means living by the common-sense ambiguity of the publicness in which nobody resolves upon anything. It means merely following the decisions made by the 'they.' On the contrary, resoluteness is letting oneself be summoned out of one's lostness in the public. It discloses to Dasein the truth that it is lost in the 'they' and gives it an authentic transparency about itself.

Resoluteness or resolution is not in a vacuum but in a *situation*. It is not a withdrawal from 'actuality' and definite possibilities. Resolution discovers what is factically possible by seizing upon it as its ownmost potentiality-for-Being. Thus the existential attributes of a resolute Dasein constitute a phenomenon called *situation*. Situation generally signifies spatiality of being in a situation. But the spatiality that belongs to Dasein's situation is grounded in its state of Being-in-the-world. Dasein's situation has its foundation in resoluteness. The situation is the 'there' which is disclosed in resoluteness. The situation is not a framework present-at-hand in which Dasein occurs. It is a mixture of circumstances and accidents which we encounter. It is only in and through resoluteness that situation is meaningful (*BT* 346). The call of conscience does indeed call us forth into the situation. The call of conscience, as resoluteness, brings the Being of the 'there' into the existence of its Situation. Heidegger maintains that resoluteness should not be mistaken for an empty '*habitus*.' Resoluteness does not first take cognizance of a Situation and later put it before itself. As Being-in-the-world, Dasein has already put itself into that Situation. Resoluteness is essentially a phenomenon of Care which defines Dasein as Being-ahead-of-itself authentically. "Resoluteness, however, is only that authenticity which, in Care, is the object of Care (*in der Sorge gesorgte*), and which is possible as Care—the authenticity of Care itself" (*BT* 348).

E. Dasein and Temporality

Besides Care, death, and authenticity, temporality is another phenomenon which forms the primordial ontological basis for Dasein's existentiality. The structural totality of Dasein's Being as Care becomes existentially intelligible only when it is demonstrated in terms of temporality. The ontological structures of Dasein which we have already obtained must be interpreted in their temporal meaning. And the phenomenon of temporality itself must be made more transparent. Then it becomes intelligible that it is only in terms of temporality that Dasein is a historical Being which can also develop histereology. As Blackham puts it, "Personal existence as a temporal process is historical and makes history."[2] Since temporality constitutes the primordial meaning of Dasein's Being, the phenomenon of Care must reckon with 'time.' The time which we experience in such reckoning is closest to us. It is out of this time that our ordinary everyday understanding of time arises. And it is this understanding of time that evolves into the traditional conception of time. Heidegger says that it is 'in' time that entities within-the-world are encountered. So it is necessary to throw light on the source of time and demonstrate time as "within-the-timeness." Thereby we have to bring to light an essential possibility of the temporalizing of temporality. It is in the primordial temporalizing of temporality that the understanding of Being which is constitutive of the Being of Dasein is grounded. It is within the horizon of time that the meaning of Being in general can be revealed.[3]

We have so far ontologically analysed the phenomenon of Dasein's authentic potentiality-for-Being-a-whole. We have existentially interpreted this phenomenon as resoluteness. We have also shown that Dasein's authentic Being-towards-death is anticipation. We now have to interpret the ontological meaning of Care by bringing together the phenomena of anticipation and resoluteness. We have to bring them together by showing that resoluteness becomes authentic by projecting itself as the anticipation of death. And it is in the phenomenon of anticipatory resoluteness that Dasein's potentiality-for-Being-a-whole becomes authentic. It is in the mode of anticipatory resoluteness that Dasein is liberated *for* its uttermost possibilities of existence. This is what Heidegger calls the existential constitution of Dasein. He also holds that the ontological meaning of the phenomenon of Care must be clarified on the basis of the existential constitution of Dasein. He contends that the determination of the ontological meaning of Care brings temporality into light. Temporality gets experienced in Dasein's authentic Being-a-whole which is the same as its anticipatory resoluteness. Temporality reveals itself in a phenomenally primordial way. Temporality as revealed in anticipatory resoluteness constitutes a distinctive mode of Dasein. The exposition of temporality through the analysis of the ontological meaning of Care gives us a full conception of Dasein's existential constitution.

Temporality has different possibilities and it temporalizes itself in different ways. Authenticity and inauthenticity are the two basic possibilities which arise out of the temporalization of temporality. The primordial phenomenon of temporality can be ascertained by analyzing the fundamental structures of Dasein in terms of time. The structures have to be developed in their totality and unity, and be conceived as being basically temporal. They have to be regarded as the basic modes of temporalizing of temporality. That is, exposition of temporality involves the interpretation of the essential structures of Dasein in terms of their temporality.

F. Anticipatory Resoluteness and Temporality

Anticipatory resoluteness arises when existence projects itself in its primordial existentiality. It makes possible Dasein's authentic Being-a-whole and signifies its Being towards its distinctive potentiality-for-Being. This is possible because Dasein comes towards itself as its ownmost possibility of letting-itself-come-towards-itself which signifies "the *future as coming to-*

wards."[4] And Dasein's Being-towards-death also signifies the future as coming towards Dasein, since Being-towards-death is possible only as something *futural* (*als Zukunfliges).* That is, anticipatory resoluteness makes Dasein *authentically* futural. Heidegger says that anticipatory resoluteness reveals not only Dasein's future but also its past, since it understands Dasein in its own essential Being-guilty. That is, it makes Dasein to *take over the* possibility of Being-guilty. Taking over the possibility of Being-guilty also means taking over thrownness.[5] Taking over thrownness signifies the Being of Dasein as it already was. This is possible "only in such a way that the futural Dasein can *be* its ownmost 'as-it-already-was,' that is to say, its 'been' (*sein Gewesen*)" (*BT* 373). The character of 'having been' arises from the future. Dasein can be authentically as 'having been' only in so far as it is futural. Similarly as authentically futural, Dasein is authentically as 'having been.' Heidegger holds that anticipatory resoluteness reveals Dasein's *present* also. It reveals the present by making what is ready-to-hand in the Situation *present.* It is only as the *present* (*Gegenwart*) in the sense of making such an entity *present* that anticipatory resoluteness can be what it is. That is, it is only by letting itself be encountered undisguisedly by an entity which is ready-to-hand that anticipatory resoluteness makes itself as the Present. It brings itself into the Situation by making itself present. It does so by coming back to itself futurally. As we have already seen, the character of "having been" also arises from the future. It arises in such a way that the future, which is in the process of having been, releases from itself the Present. Temporality thus implies the anticipatory resoluteness which unifies the three temporal modes, namely, the having been, the present and the future. "This phenomenon has the unity of a future which makes present in the process of having been; we designate it as temporality" (*BT* 374), avers Heidegger.

The meaning of temporality as drawn from the state of Being of anticipatory resoluteness is different from the ordinary conception of time. The conception of the past, present and future as ordinarily understood does not represent the existential conception of temporality. Even the 'subjective,' the 'objective,' 'immanent' or 'transcendent' conceptions of time do not signify the temporality of anticipatory resoluteness. The ordinary conceptions of time are derivative in character. They arise out of an inauthentic way of understanding time. The inauthentic temporality has its source in temporality which is authentic and primordial. The authentic and primordial phenomenon of time arises out of anticipatory resoluteness which signifies Dasein's Being as Care. Dasein's Being as Care signifies its structural totality which is ahead-of-itself-already-being-in-a world as Being-alongside entities encountered within-the-world. Heidegger says that the primordial unity of the structure of Care lies in temporality. That is, the 'ahead-of-itself' is grounded in the future; the 'Being-already-in' signifies the 'having been'; and 'Being-alongside' is possible in making present. The terms "ahead" and "already" should not be taken in terms of the way time is ordinarily understood. "Ahead" does not mean 'in advance of something'; 'already' does not mean 'no longer now, but earlier.' If these terms were to have these meanings then Care would be something which is 'earlier' and 'later'; Care would then be an entity which occurs and runs its course 'in time.' Then Dasein would be reduced to something present-at-hand. This cannot be the case. So the term 'ahead' should be taken to mean the kind of the future which would make Dasein's Being such that its potentiality-for-Being is an issue. Similarly, the term "already" signifies Dasein's existential situation of having already been thrown. Dasein exists as the thrown entity, since Care is based on the character of 'having been.' As the Being of Care, Dasein is never past (*Vergangen*) but it always is as already having *been*. Dasein always finds itself as a thrown fact. In the state-of-mind in which Dasein finds itself, it finds itself as the entity which it still is and already was. That is, Dasein constantly *is* as having been. Thus the terms "ahead" and "already" have to be understood in their primordial meaning. The former signifies Dasein's essential characteristic of existentiality. The latter signifies Dasein's primary existential meaning of facticity. Heidegger says, "In our formulation of the structure of Care, the temporal meaning of existentiality and facticity is indicated by the expressions "ahead" (before) and "already" (*BT* 376).

And the third item which constitutes Care, namely, the "Being-alongside" is also grounded in temporality. The "Being-alongside" signifies the *present* which stands for Dasein's state of falling. It is included in the future and in "having been." Thus temporality constitutes the unity of existence, facticity and falling. It constitutes the totality of Care. These three temporal items of Care are not separate pieces tied together *in* a cumulative manner. So also temporality is not put together in the course of time (*mit der zeit*). Temporality is composed by the future, the having been and the present. It arises by temporalizing itself in the different possible ways of itself. These ways make possible the multiplicity of Dasein's modes of Being. They also make possible Dasein's basic possibilities of authentic and inauthentic existence (*BT* 377).

As it has been mentioned above the items of temporality—the future, the having been and the present—are not entities which constitute the entity of temporality. They are the *ecstases*[6] which reveal Dasein's phenomenal characteristics of the 'towards-oneself,' the 'back-to' and the 'letting-oneself-be-encountered-by[7]. Temporality is the pure, simple and primordial 'out-side-of-itself' in and for-itself. It is not an entity which emerges out of itself but a process of temporalizing in the unity of the ecastases. This is the primordial and existential conception of time which forms the basis for the common sense understanding of time as a pure sequence of 'nows' without beginning and end. The time which is accessible to the ordinary understanding is that in which the ecstatical character of primordiality has been levelled off. This levelling off the ecstatical character implies temporality temporalizing itself in an inauthentic way. The primordial time alone is the authentic time. It is out of this time that the inauthentic time which is accessible to Dasein's common sense arises. Of the three ecstases, the future has priority over the other two. It is primarily in terms of the authentic future that authentic temporality temporalizes itself. It is in having been futurally that the authentic temporality first of all awakens the present. Heidegger therefore says that the authentic future is temporalized by the temporality which is of anticipatory resoluteness. Heidegger therefore says that the primary phenomenon of primordial and authentic temporality is the future.[8]

According to Heidegger temporality is finite. Its finitude consists in its primordial and authentic future which is finite. Future is finite since it signifies Dasein's "coming-towards-itself"; it signifies Dasein's existence as the possibility of nullity, which is not to be outstripped. The ecstatical character of the future lies in the fact that the future closes one's potentiality-for-Being. It makes possible the resolute existentiell understanding of nullity. That is, future as authentic coming-towards-oneself means existing in one's ownmost nullity. "Primordial and authentic coming-towards-oneself is the meaning of existing in one's ownmost nullity."[9] Temporality therefore is primordially finite, although 'time goes on' and everything can still happen in it. Time is finite simply because Dasein's primordial existential projecting into future is finite. The idea that time is infinite and endless is confined to the ordinary way of understanding. It is not a primordial but only a derived inauthentic conception of time. It is only because primordial time is *finite* that the 'derived' time temporalizes itself as *infinite*.[10].

G. Temporality and Everydayness

With the analysis of temporality carried out so far, we have arrived at the primordial, the existential conception of temporality as a phenomenon. It is on the basis of the primordial phenomenon of time that time as within-the-timeness arises. Time as within-the-timeness signifies the temporal attribute of the entities within-the-world. Dasein is an entity which is within-the-world. Being-in-the-world is its everydayness which is always within-the-timeness. So there is a need for a temporal interpretation of everyday Dasein. The interpretation must start with the items in which disclosedness constitutes itself. The items in which temporality temporalizes itself should be analyzed. This analysis will help us in defining the temporality of Being-in-the-world of all entities and Dasein in particular.

Interpretation of everydayness in terms of temporality warrants an analysis of the temporal constitution of Care. It means we have to give a temporal interpretation of the items of the structure of Care. The items are (i) understanding; (ii) state-of-mind; (iii) falling, and (iv) discourse. The temporal constitution of these items will show that they are united in their structure. Every understanding has its mood. Every state-of-mind is one in which one understands. The understanding which one has in such a state-of-mind has the character of falling. And the understanding which has its mood attained in falling, articulates itself in discourse. Thus the temporal interpretation of these items will reveal a single kind of temporality in which they are united.

(i) The Temporality of Understanding

As it has already been mentioned, understanding is not cognition in the sense of grasping something thematically. Understanding is a fundamental *existentiale* which constitutes Dasein's Being of the 'there.' It is on the basis of this kind of understanding that Dasein develops the different possibilities of sight, looking around, and just looking. The term "understanding," in its primordially existential sense, means "to be projecting towards a potentiality-for-Being for the sake of which any Dasein exists" (*BT* 385). In understanding, one's own potentiality-for-Being is disclosed in such a way that one's Dasein always knows understandingly what it is capable of. Explanation is uncovering understandingly that which one cannot easily understand. All explanation is thus rooted in Dasein's primary understanding. And it is through the ecstases of future that Dasein can understand itself projectively as coming towards-oneself. "The future makes ontologically possible an entity which is in such a way that it exists understandingly in its potentiality-for-Being" (*BT* 385). Heidegger designates authentic future as anticipation. In authentic future, Dasein exists authentically and lets itself come towards itself as its ownmost potentiality-for-Being. This is possible because Dasein, as a Being of Care, is constantly ahead-of-itself. The term "ahead-of-itself" thus is synonymous with the term "future."

(ii) The Temporality of State-of-Mind

Understanding is never free-floating but always goes with a state-of-mind. "Being-thrown" is Dasein's fundamental state of Being. It means that Dasein always finds itself in some state-of-mind or other. Dasein's state-of-mind is thus based upon thrownness which is represented by its mood. The mood is disclosed in the manner in which Dasein turns away from itself. Dasein is brought face to face with the "that-it-is" of its own thrownness. This is possible only if Dasein's Being is constantly 'having been.' The 'been' is not what first brings Dasein face to face with its thrownness. The 'been' is the ecstases which first makes it possible to find Dasein in the way of having a state-of-mind. Thus Dasein's state-of-mind temporalizes itself *primarily* in *having been*. The other two ecstases, namely, the future and the present, are modified by 'having been' (*BT* 390). So one's state of mind is grounded in 'having been.' It means that the basic existential character of mood lies in *bringing* Dasein back to something. This bringing-back does not first produce a having been but the having been is made manifest in a state-of-mind.

This becomes evident only in an existential analysis of the state-of-mind. Heidegger says that both fear and anxiety have a temporal character. As modes of state-of-mind they are grounded in the ecstases of 'having been.' But they have different sources of temporalization in the temporality of Care. Fear springs from the lost present, while anxiety arises out of the future of resoluteness. According to Heidegger the other modes of state-of-mind like hope, joy, enthusiasm, gaiety, satiety, sadness, melancholy and desperation are temporal, since they are founded upon Dasein's having been (*BT* 395).

(iii) The Temporality of Falling

The temporal interpretation of the phenomenon of understanding has revealed the ecstases of future. The temporal interpretation of the phenomenon of state-of-mind has revealed another ecstases, namely, the 'having been.' And the third constitutive item of care, namely falling will reveal the third ecstases, namely, the *present.* Falling is represented by idle talk, curiosity and ambiguity. But it is in the phenomenon of curiosity that the temporality of falling is most evident. Curiosity is a distinctive tendency of Dasein's Being. It is in accordance with this tendency that Dasein concerns itself with a potentiality-for-seeing. Seeing is not restricted to awareness through the eyes of the body. Awareness in the broader sense lets what is ready-to-hand and what is present-at-hand be encountered 'bodily' in themselves. It lets them be encountered in the way they look. Letting them be thus encountered is grounded in a *present.* This present is the ecstatical horizon within which entities can have bodily *presence.* Thus curiosity makes *present* the present-at-hand and the ready-to-hand. In making them present, curiosity has an ecstatical unity with a corresponding future and a corresponding 'having been.' Curiosity has a corresponding future, since it always holds by what is coming next; it has a corresponding 'having been,' since it holds also by forgetting what has gone before (*BT* 399).

(iv) The Temporality of Discourse

Discourse is the Articulation of the disclosedness of Dasein's Being-there-which is constituted by understanding, state-of-mind, and falling. Discourse expresses itself for the most part in language. It talks about things concernfully and makes them *present*. This *making-present* has a privileged constitutive function. Discourse does not temporalize itself primarily in any definite ecstases. But discourse *in itself* is temporal, since all talking about is grounded in the ecstatical unity of temporality (*BT* 400).

Thus temporality temporalizes itself as a whole in every ecstases: understanding is grounded primarily in the future; states-of-mind temporalize themselves primarily in 'having been'; and falling has its roots in the present. At the same time, understanding is in every case a present which is in the process of 'having been'; one's state-of-mind temporalizes itself, as a future which is 'making present'; and the present 'leaps away' from a future that is in the process of 'having been.' This also shows that the structural whole of existence, facticity, and falling which constitute Care is grounded in the ecstatical unity with which temporality temporalizes itself (*BT* 401).

H. The Temporality of Being-in-the-World and the Transcendence of the World

As it has already been mentioned Being-in-the-world is the basic state of Dasein's existence. It has such a structural unity that it cannot be torn apart. The unity has been exhibited in the analysis of its everyday mode, namely, concernful Being-alongside-the ready-to-hand within-the-world. So, now the phenomenon of 'concern' has to be conceived in terms of temporality for obtaining the temporal interpretation of Being-in-the-world. This involves an analysis of the phenomenon of concern in two ways: (i) the temporality of circumspective concern; (ii) the temporal meaning of the circumspective deliberation. Besides this the transcendence of the world must also be considered in terms of temporality. Only then the existential-temporal interpretation of Being-in-the-world will be complete.

(i) The Temporality of Circumspective Concern

Concernful Being-alongside the 'world' is called 'dealings' in and with the environment. The using, manipulation, and producing of the ready-to-hand are the examples of Being-alongside-the world. The deficient and undifferentiated modes of the using, manipulation and producing are also the examples of Being-alongside-the-world. These are the ways of concernful Being-alongside-the-world. They also belong to one's everyday needs. Dasein's authentic existence maintains itself in this kind of concernful Being. The ready-to-hand things are those with which we concern ourselves. But they are not the causes of our concern. Concern does not arise out of the effects of the entities within-the-world. Heidegger says that Being-alongside cannot be explained ontically in terms of the ready-to-hand. So also the ready-to-hand cannot be derived from the Being alongside. Neither the Being-alongside nor the ready-to-hand is concern. But there is a connection subsisting between them. They constitute a kind of Being which belongs to Dasein. We concern ourselves with this Being as something ready-to-hand within-the-world. We concern ourselves with it as something which is *just present-at-hand together* (*BT* 403).

That which is dealt with sheds light upon concernful dealings. The phenomenal structure of what is dealt with reveals the existential constitution of dealings. Cocnernful dealings do not dwell in any individual item of equipment. The using and manipulating of a definite item of equipment are always oriented towards some equipmental content. For instance, in searching for some equipment which is 'misplaced' what we have in mind is not merely what we are searching for; we do not have it in mind in an isolated 'act.' What we indeed have in mind is the range of the equipmental totality which is discovered before-hand. So also, whenever we take hold of something to work with, we do not seize it out from 'nothing'; we do not come upon it as something which has been presented to us in isolation. Instead we take hold of it as an item of equipment from out of the work-world that has already been disclosed (*BT* 404).

The above analysis shows that one's existent Being alongside the entities must be given an orientation towards the equipmental totality. This way of understanding what is dealt with, arises out of the consideration of the character of Being which belongs to *involvement*. Ontologically, to say that something has *with* it an involvement *in* something is to indicate the kind of Being that belongs to what is ready-to-hand. Involvement has a relational character which suggests that ontologically there can be no such thing as 'an' equipment. Everything that is ready-to-hand belongs *to* something else. Our concernful dealings reveal the ready-to-hand circumspectively only when we understand them in terms of involvement. The Being-alongside discovers the ready-to-hand circumspectively in concern. It lets the ready-to-hand be involved. That is, it projects an involvement understandingly. Heidegger says that this possibility of letting things be involved must be sought in a mode of temporality. Letting things be involved makes up the structure of concern which as Being alongside something belongs to the essential constitution of Care which in turn, is grounded in temporality. So the existential condition of the possibility of letting things be involved must be sought in a mode of temporalizing of temporality (*BT* 404).

(ii) Temporality and Circumspective Deliberation

Here Heidegger tries to clarify the meaning of Being and the 'connection' between Being and truth. He tries to interpret them in terms of the temporality of existence. To him, this is the central problematic within which the idea of phenomenology is distinguished from the preliminary conception of it. It involves the investigation of the way in which circumspective concern with the ready-to-hand is modified into an exploration of the present-at-hand within-the-world. It also involves investigation of the temporal constitution of Being-in-the-world in general.

The modes of manipulating and using are circumspective in a 'practical' way. They can be changed over to 'theoretical' exploration. Merely looking at entities emerges when concern holds back from any kind of manipulation. It means that the theoretical attitude lies in the *disappearance of praxis*. (Practical concern is the primary and predominant kind of Being which is possessed by the factical Dasein). The ontological possibility of 'theory' is due to the absence of praxis which is a *privation*. It means that theory begins when there is the discontinuance of a specific manipulation in our concernful dealings. But the discontinuance does not simply leave the circumspection behind as a remainder. Rather, the concern then diverts itself specifically into a just-looking-around (*ein Nur-sich-umsehen*). But this is not the way in which the 'theoretical' attitude of science is arrived at. On the contrary, the discontinuance of manipulation tarries for a certain length of time. The tarrying of discontinued manipulation takes on the character of a more precise kind of circumspection. The circumspection may manifest itself as 'inspecting' what has been attained. It may also manifest itself as looking over the 'operations' which are now at a standstill (*BT* 409).

As it has been already mentioned mere looking at entities emerges only when concern *holds back* from the use of equipment. This holding back is far from sheer 'theory.' So the circumspection which tarries remains completely in the grip of the ready-to-hand equipment with which one is concerned. And 'practical' dealings have their *own* ways of tarrying. Praxis has its own specific kind of theory. So also theoretical research has its own praxis. For instance, reading off the measurements drawn from an experiment requires a complicated technical knowhow. And observation with a microscope is dependent upon the production of 'preparations.' This shows that scientific behaviour is not a purely intellectual activity but a way of Being-in-the-world.

Heidegger says that the exhibition of the existential genesis of science is possible only by characterizing the *circumspection* which is the guide for 'practical concern.' Circumspection operates in the involvement-relationships of the context of equipment which is ready-to-hand. It is subordinate to the guidance of an explicit survey of equipmental totality. This survey is one in which things that are present-at-hand are subsequently scraped together. It illumines one's concern and receives its 'light' from the potentiality-for-Being for the sake of which concern exists as Care. Thus the concernful circumspection brings the ready-to-hand *closer* to Dasein. And it is by interpreting what has been sighted that the concernful circumspection brings the ready-to-hand closer to Dasein. This way of bringing the object of concern close to Dasein by interpreting it circumspectively Heidegger calls circumspective deliberation (*Uberlegung*). The deliberation requires the 'if-then' scheme. For instance if this or that is to be produced then some ways and means are required. It illumines Dasein's current factical situation with which it concerns itself. Thus the circumspective deliberation brings the environment closer. This way of bringing the environment closer in circumspective deliberation has the existential meaning of *making present* which brings in temporality. The circumspective making-present belongs to a full ecstatical unity of temporality (*BT* 410).

I. The Temporal Problem of the Transcendence of the World

In the existential analysis of Dasein, temporality occupies a central place. The importance of time becomes more evident with the analysis of the temporal dimension of the transcendence of the world. Dasein's Being is defined as Care the ontological meaning of which is temporality. Temporality constitutes the disclosedness of the 'there' in which the world is also disclosed. It implies that the ontological constitution of the world is grounded in temporality. Heidegger says, "The existential-temporal condition for the possibility of the world lies in the fact that temporality, as an ecstatical unity, has something like a horizon" (*BT* 416).

The three temporal ecstases—the past, the present and the future—signify three different directions ('whither') to which Dasein is carried away. The 'whither' which each ecstases signifies Heidegger calls the "horizontal scheme." Each ecstases has a different schema. The schema in which Dasein comes towards itself *futurally* is the for-sake-of-itself. The schema in which Dasein is disclosed in a state-of-mind is *what has been.* And Dasein's mode of in-order-to-be discloses the schema for the *present.* Thus the unity of the horizontal schema of future, the having been and the present is grounded in the ecstatical unity of temporality. The meaning of Dasein's Being-in-the-world lies in the unity of the in-order-to (*Um-Zn*), the for-the-sake-of-which (*Worumwillen*), and in-the-face-of-which (*wovor*). These three ecstases provide the horizon of the ecstases of temporality. And the world is revealed as Dasein temporalizes itself in the unity of these three ecstases. The world is not an aggregate of the objects encountered within the world. It is transcendent to the multiplicity of entities as well as to the subject-object dichotomy. The world has its ground (*grundend*) in the horizontal unity of ecstatical temporality. As a transcendent entity, the world makes the entities to be encountered within it. "Together with the 'there'—disclosedness—of Dasein, the entities too are encountered. This is enabled by the transcendence of the world, grounded in the horizontal unity of ecstatical temporality."[11]

J. The Temporality of Dasein's Spatiality and Everydayness

Spatiality is one of Dasein's basic attributes which correspond to its temporality. The existential-temporal analysis of Dasein becomes almost complete with the consideration of Dasein's spatiality. Dasein's spatiality does not mean that Dasein is in space. So Dasein's temporality does not signify that Dasein is in time, but it signifies Dasein's Being of Care. Dasein's constitution and its ways are possible only on the basis of temporality. So Dasein's specific spatiality is grounded in temporality. Spatiality is existentially possible only through temporality. It does not mean that spatiality is deduced from time. It only means that spatiality is existentially grounded in temporality.[12] As it has been mentioned, Dasein can be spatial only as Care. It means that Dasein is never present-at-hand in space. Dasein does not occupy a bit of space as a real Thing. It is by no means present-at-hand in a bit of space which its body occupies. Dasein takes space *in,* which means that Dasein is not a physical but a 'spiritual' entity. It is only because Dasein is spiritual that "it can be spatial in a way which remains essentially impossible for any extended corporeal Thing" (*BT* 419).

Everydayness is the kind of Being in which Dasein maintains itself proximally and for the most part. It stands for the way of existing in which Dasein maintains itself everyday. Here everydayness does not signify the sum of the days Dasein lives in its lifetime. It is not to be understood calendrically either. Yet everydayness has a temporal character. It signifies the 'how' of Dasein's existence by which it is dominated through and through for life (*Zeitlebens*). The 'how' is that in accordance with which Dasein 'lives unto the day' in all its ways of behaving. It signifies the comfortableness of the accustomed. That is, in everydayness everything is all one and the same. Everydayness is a way *to be* to which that which is publicly manifest belongs. It is more or less a familiar phenomenon to any individual Dasein. It is familiar to Dasein as a way of existing which Dasein may have as its own. Everydayness is familiar to Dasein through its own state-of-mind and Dasein in its everydayness *stretches* itself along temporally. Heidegger says, "The 'it is all one and the same,' the 'accustomed,' the 'like yesterday, so today and to-morrow' and the 'for the most part'—these are not to be grasped without recourse to this 'temporal' stretching-along of Dasein" (*BT* 423).

Thus Heidegger throws light on temporality as the ontological meaning of Dasein's Being. With this the existential analytic of Dasein reaches its zenith. But this is only a formal structure of Dasein's temporality. There is a need for the concretization of the formal structure through the analysis of Dasein's historicality.

K. Temporality and Historicality

Heidegger takes up the issue of historicality in order to concretize the formal structure of the temporality of Dasein. The ontological understanding of historicality (*Geschichtlichkeit*) is possible through the analysis of Dasein's structure of historizing. The analysis of the existential-temporal conditions of the possibility of historizing is necessary for understanding of Dasein's historicality. Historizing is the specific movement in which Dasein stretches itself along between its birth and death. The stretch of Dasein's life between birth and death is not filled up with successive experiences of life. Dasein stretches itself along in such a way that its own Being is constituted in advance, as a stretching-along. The temporal element of 'between' lies in the very heart of Dasein and it relates to both birth and death. It does not imply that 'now' alone is actual and birth and death are non-actual. In its existential sense birth is not anything 'no-more';

nor is death anything 'not-yet.' Instead, birth and death are actualities which temporally or historically determine Dasein's Being. Factically Dasein exists as born, and having been born it is already dying. The moment Dasein is born it is already a being-towards-death. "As long as Dasein factically exists, both the 'ends' and their 'between' *are*, and they *are* in the only way which is possible on the basis of Dasein's Being as care."[13]

According to Heidegger, ontological constitution of Dasein's historicality is different from the ordinary understanding of 'history.' We call something historical in so far as it belongs to a world of Dasein which is primarily historical. Dasein is the only entity that is historical since it alone exists in the temporal mode of *having been*. The other entities are historical only in a secondary sense. The ordinary, everyday conception of history is founded on three notions, viz., Dasein, world and time with a priority of the 'past.' The analysis of these notions constitutes the background for the exposition of historicality.[14]

Historicality is centred primarily on Dasein. So the constitution of historicality must be sought in temporality. Temporality consists in Dasein's authentic existence which is revealed in anticipatory resoluteness. So historicality implies an authentic historizing of Dasein. Historizing is the filling in of existence between birth and death by realizing the existentiell possibilities. It is a process of temporalizing between birth and death. Historizing cannot be understood in terms of the successive moments called 'nows.' The 'nows,' according to Heidegger, constitute the inauthentic conception of time. Realization of existentiell possibilities is not a process of fragmentary and successive events. On the contrary, realization of existentiell possibilities is a self-stretching between birth and death. It is a single and unitary happening which is called historizing (*Geschehen*).

Dasein's authentic historizing takes place in the following way. As we have already seen, Dasein is thrown into the world where it factically exists with Others. In its everyday, indifferent mode, Dasein finds itself in the heritage (*Erbe*) of its being-in-the-world. In this mode Dasein's authentic possibilities are unrecognizable. It exists in ambiguity and understands itself in terms of the public way of interpreting its possibilities. But Dasein as a Being of resoluteness discloses its factical possibilities of authentic existence in terms of 'heritage.' "Heritage is the whole of the 'givenness' that Dasein, as to-be-in-the-world, is with. The authentically existing Dasein, in taking over its heritage, understands and historizes itself in terms of 'fate' (*Schicksal*) and 'destiny" (*Geschik*)."[15]

Fate, according to Heidegger, is the awareness of finitude in one's given factical possibilities. Destiny is the social dimension of the finite givenness. The resolute Dasein, existing in intersubjective community shares the finitude of the community. So fate and destiny are interrelated. This shows that Dasein's historizing lies in its authentic resoluteness. It lies in a possibility in which Dasein hands itself down to itself, free for death. It also consists in a possibility which Dasein has inherited and yet has chosen. In its authentic resoluteness, Dasein anticipates its death and understands itself in terms of its ownmost distinctive possibility. In it, Dasein chooses and finds the possibility of its existence. But this choice is a finite one, since it chooses the inherited possibility. Thus Dasein grasps its finitude and brings itself away from the multiplicity of comfortable possibilities. It assumes the simplicity of its fate which is both given as well as chosen. The fateful Dasein is essentially Being-with-others. So its historizing is a co-historizing in terms of destiny which becomes free only in Dasein's communication with Others. "Dasein's fateful destiny in and with its 'generation' goes to make up the full authentic historizing of Dasein."[16]

As a Being of historicality Dasein hands down a possibility that has been inherited. In such handing down, Dasein repeats a possibility of its existence. Repeating is going back into the possibilities. And the authentic repetition of a possibility that has been is grounded in anticipatory resoluteness. Repetition is a matter of reclamation rather than recurrence. What is reclaimed are possibilities rather than factual historical incidents. It is through repetition that the past takes on meaning. Devoid of repetition, past remains to be a mere collection of meaningless and isolated facts. "The hidden and primordial meanings, embedded in one's tradition are uncovered when one projectively understands the past—understanding is always in terms of the projection of possibilities."[17]

The historizing Dasein is not a worldless subject but an entity that is to-be-in-the-world. Dasein in its historizing deals with the environmental and communal world. It exists through human undertakings and natural processes. Hence historizing of Dasein includes all that is concerned with its existence in the world. Thus it may be said that Dasein's historicality is essentially the historicality of the world in temporality. So Dasein as historical has the world-historical as its complement. The phrase 'world-historical' signifies the historizing of the world in its essential unity of Dasein. It also signifies the historizing of the entities with-in-the world. In this sense even the natural events too belong to the world-historical. Dasein's approach to the world-historical may be authentic or inauthentic. Dasein's authentic approach to the world-historical signifies Dasein's resoluteness for its Self. It incorporates into its existence birth and death and their 'between.' Dasein accepts the thrownness of its own 'there' by stretching back from its possibility of death to the heritage given with its birth. Dasein understands history as a recurrence of the possible. It knows that a possibility will recur only if existence is open for it in resolute repetition. Heidegger calls this as the authentic historicality which is also primordial. It is founded on the ecstatio-horizontal temporality. It includes the world-historical into Dasein's historizing which is stretching along birth and death. Unlike the authentic approach, the inauthentic approach to the world historical consists in Dasein's being blind to its character of stretching-along. Here, Dasein historizes itself in terms of 'today' and is laden with the legacy of the past. It reckons with the 'mute' facts of the present and is satisfied with the conventionalities of the 'they.' It only lives on the 'left over' of the world historical and is oblivious to the inherited possibilities which can be repeatable.[18]

To sum up the discussion, we have analyzed Dasein's potentiality-for-Being something for which authentic existence is possible. We have explicated conscience as the phenomenon which presents Dasein in its authentic potentiality-for-Being. Conscience as the call of Care has been explained in all its dimensions. A clear distinction has been made between the existential interpretation of conscience and the way it is ordinarily interpreted. We have also explained resoluteness as a phenomenon of Care which defines Dasein as Being-ahead-of-itself authentically. Further, temporality as the primordial ontological basis of Dasein's existentiality has been examined. Dasein's Being as Care is made intelligible by demonstrating it in terms of temporality. The temporal process of Dasein's Being is exhibited by interpreting its ontological structures in their temporal meaning. Thus the existential-ontological interpretation of the Being of Dasein in all its structures comes to a close. And the task of answering the question of the meaning of Being in its totality gets accomplished.

NOTES

1. Martin Heidegger, *Being and Time*. Trans. John Macquarie & Edward Robinson, Basil Blackwell, Oxford, 1978, p. 276.
2. H.J. Blackham, *Six Existentialist Thinkers*. Routledge & Kegan Paul, London, 1961, p. 100.
3. *Ibid.*, p, 99.
4. Johnson J. Puthenpurackal, *Heidegger through Authentic Totality to Total Authenticity*—A unitary Approach to his thought in its

two phases. Louvain philosophical studies-2, Leuven University Press, 1987, p. 67.

5. *Ibid.*, p. 68.
6. Here the term "ecstases" should not be understood in the traditional sense of mystic ecstasy. It should also not to be understood in its literal meaning of something standing beside itself (*ausser-sich*). According to Heidegger, ecstasy signifies Dasein's triadic temporal dimension of the past, present and future.
7. Herbert Spiegelberg, *Phenomenological Movement—A Historical Introduction.* Vol. I, Mortinus Nijhoff, The Hague, 1961, p. 334.
8. *Ibid.*, pp. 335-36.
9. Johnson J. Puthenpurackal, p. 71.
10. *Ibid.*, p. 72.
11. *Ibid.*, p. 72.
12. In this Heidegger does not subscribe to Kant's view that time is prior to space. He does not accept the idea that space is deduced from pure time.
13. Johnson J. Puthenpurackal, p. 75.
14. *Ibid.*, p. 76.
15. *Ibid.*
16. *Ibid.*, p. 77.
17. *Ibid.*, p. 78.
18. *Ibid.*, p. 79.

Chapter VI

Conclusion

Heidegger is one of the greatest metaphysicians of the twentieth century. His main task in his *Being and Time* is to answer the question of the meaning of Being in its totality. He has tried to answer the question by adopting a method called phenomenology. And the being through which he tried to accomplish the task is Dasein or human reality which is closest in its relation to Being. Being, according to Heidegger, is not what-is; it is not brute existent either; it is not even Plato's Idea of the good; nor is it Aristotle's Unmoved Mover; nor is it Anselm's God of whom nothing greater can be conceived. Unlike the notion of Being in Western tradition, which is onto-theological in character, Heidegger's concept of Being is not an entity as such but it is the Being of entities and of Dasein which are very much Being-in-the-world. Being is the most universal and self-evident concept which cannot be defined in terms of the 'abstractions' of formal logic. It cannot be dealt with by the ancient ontology which confined itself to the entities which do not have the character of Dasein. Being, in its primordiality, can be adequately interpreted only by the hermeneutic of Dasein which has both ontical and ontological priority over all other beings to the disclosure of Being. Only philosophy as a universal phenomenological ontology can disclose Being in its totality by disclosing the structures of Dasein's Being as a whole. In other words, philosophy as fundamental ontology alone can unravel Being through the constitution the Being of Dasein. It is only through philosophy as the analytic of *existence* that Being can be fully conceived. Heidegger, at the same time, holds that ancient ontology and its formal logic with its abstractions and thing-concepts can not be totally dispensed with. They should be taken as the point of departure for fundamental ontology which alone can properly formulate and clarify the question of the meaning of Being.

In this study, we have ventured to disclose Being by disclosing the Being which belongs to existent Dasein as a way in which it understands Being. We have tried to accomplish the task of uncovering Being by interpreting Dasein as Being-in-the-world, as Being of care and death, and as Being of authenticity and temporality. It is in the process of unravelling the meaning of Being that Dasein gets unravelled. Or rather, it is in the process of unravelling the Being of Dasein that the meaning of Being as such is unravelled. That is why, the question of the meaning of Being is clarified before taking up the ontological-existential interpretation of Dasein in all its dimensions. The whole discussion has been carried out in four main chapters, besides Introduction and Conclusion which, respectively, constitute Chapter I and Chapter VI.

In Chapter II we have elaborated the nature and content of the question of the meaning of Being. A justification has been given for Heidegger's claim that the question of the meaning of Being should be taken as a theme for phenomenological investigation. The presuppositions of ancient ontology about the question of the meaning of Being have been explained; the ontical and ontological priority of the question and its formal structure have been analyzed. Further, the ontological analytic of Dasein and its three-fold priority to the question of the meaning of Being have been elaborated. Temporality has been explicated as the horizon for understanding and interpreting Being as the Being of Dasein. Heidegger's critique of the history of ontology has been presented and in the process we have also shown how Dasein is essentially a Being of historicality. We have concluded the chapter with a detailed exposition of the phenomenological method which Heidegger formulates as 'to the things themselves,' and which he advocates as the best suitable method for interpreting Being through the analytic of Dasein.

In Chapter III, the structure of Being-in-the-world which constitutes the very Being of Dasein has been analyzed in great detail. The constituent items of Being-in-the-world, namely, 'Being-in,' Dasein and 'the world' have been interpreted in ontological and existential terms. The ideas of the worldhood of the world, its environmentality and its various manifestations like reference, assignment, involvement and significance have been analyzed. A clear-cut distinction has been made between Heidegger's and Descartes' interpretation of the world. Further, Dasein as the entity which has Being-in-the-world as a way of its Being has been elucidated in all its dimensions like the 'who' of Dasein, Dasein-with Others and its everyday Being-one's self. The structure of the Being-in as such along with its constituent items like knowing the world, and the state-of-mind as thrownness, fear, understanding, interpretation and assertion, discourse and language have been elucidated. And Dasein's everyday Being-there has been explicated in all its aspects like idle talk, curiosity, ambiguity and falling.

In Chapter IV, we have dealt with Dasein's Being as care and as Being towards death. We have shown that the phenomenon of anxiety, which is Dasein's basic state of mind, discloses Dasein as Being of care. Being-ahead-of-itself-being-already-in-the-world alongside the entities encountered within-the-world has been interpreted as Dasein's Being as care. Truth and reality have been elucidated in the light of the phenomenon of care. We have explained reality as being grounded in the Being of Dasein as care, and truth as the uncovering of the Being of Dasein as care. Heidegger's contention that in the absence of Dasein the phenomena of reality and truth are meaningless, has been explained. A detailed account of the ontological method of interpretation and its hermeneutical situation has been given. Next we have explained death as Dasein's ownmost possibility of its Being-in-the-world. With death Dasein stands before itself in a non-relational potentiality-for-Being. Death is Dasein's facticity into which it is thrown and which Dasein can never outstrip. Besides presenting Dasein's Being-towards-Death in its everydayness, a full account of the existential-ontological conception of Dasein's authentic Being-towards-death also has been elucidated.

In Chapter V, we have discussed authenticity as a possibility for Dasein's potentiality-for-Being. Conscience as Dasein's call of care and as its authentic potentiality-for-Being has been explicated. The existential interpretation of conscience has been distinguished from its ordinary interpretation. Resoluteness as the phenomenon of care has been explained in detail. Further, temporality is interpreted as the primordial basis of Dasein's existentiality. Dasein's Being as care is interpreted in terms of temporality. Dasein's Being as a whole is shown to be a temporal and finite process by interpreting all its structures in their temporal meaning. Thus the existential-ontological hermeneutic of Dasein as a whole comes to an end. Thereby the task of explicating the meaning of Being in its totality is completed.

Let us now turn our attention to a critical appraisal of Heidegger's thought. On the whole Heidegger's work is voluminous. His thinking stretches along three score years of his life and spreads through numerous works. It weaves together several themes and standpoints. It embodies obscure way-makings, abstruse 'foot paths' and untrodden 'forest-trails' of reflection. Heidegger's thinking also had its ups and downs as well as an evident turn (*Kehre*) of standpoints. But our study is confined to Heidegger's thought as contained in his major work, *Being and Time*. We therefore restrict our critical observations to Heidegger's central problematic, namely, the interpretation of the question of the meaning of Being through the existential analytic of Dasein.

Firstly, let us begin our critical appraisal of Heidegger's thought by examining his notion of 'sight' (*Sicht*) in *Being and Time*. Heidegger says that Dasein's existential 'sight' is a projective understanding that shows itself in its various modes. Heidegger illustrates these modes of sight or looking in the following way. When I look at the environmental world, I employ circumspection; when I look at the communal world, I make use of considerateness, and finally, when I look into myself, I adopt transparency. Thus the term "sight" is used in the sense of looking in many directions. But yet there is a deficiency in Heidegger's use of the term. The term is not used in several other senses like looking 'upwards,' 'downwards' and 'sideways.' Since Heideggerian 'sight' lacks the dimension of the 'upward' look, Heidegger's philosophy lacks an adequate dimension of the Divine. Since the 'sight' is devoid of the 'downward' look, his philosophy is left without an adequate 'earthly' dimension. And since the 'sight' is deficient in looking 'sideways,' Heidegger's thought suffers from the lack of the horizontal dimension of dealing with intersubjectivity. Heidegger's consideration of intersubjectivity is very limited and inadequate.

Let us examine the three issues more elaborately. As the Heideggerian 'sight' does not have the dimension of the 'upward' it lacks an adequate teleology. An adequate teleology and a meaningful conception of God requires a comprehensive consideration of intersubjectivity. It also requires the acceptance of God as the irreducible Other. It is only through the full understanding of the finite 'thous' of intersubjectivity that one is able to look upward to the Absolute Thou. But Heidegger's treatment of intersubjectivity is far too minimal. He admits that Dasein as Being-in-the-world is Being-with-others also. But he has given the equipmental world of ready-to-hand more importance than to the communal world of Daseins. His analysis of Dasein in its concernful dealings with the ready-to-hand entities occupies more space in *Being and Time.* His analysis of other Daseins is overshadowed by the analysis of the equipmental mediation. To Heidegger Dasein's relation to the equipmental world is primary, whereas, its relation to the intersubjective community is only secondary. The former is frontal while the latter is lateral only. To him, everyday dealings with the ready-to-hand equipmental world are the general rule while a genuine everyday relationship with other persons is a rare exception. The deficient treatment of intersubjectivity is at the root of the inadequate treatment of the Divine. In *Being and Time*, Heidegger leaves out the question of God completely. Theology totally falls outside the thinking of Being. The marathon analysis of the question of the meaning of Being through the Being of Dasein is totally exclusive of the treatment of man's religious expression. The deficient treatment of the Divine leaves Heidegger's philosophy with an inadequate teleology.

Secondly, Heidegger's notion of 'sight' lacks a 'downward-look' and fails to consider man in his earthliness. That is, it is oblivious of the human person in flesh and blood—body, instincts and emotions. His notion of man's Being-in-the-world is not earthly enough and his notion of dwelling in the world is not adequately earth-bound, despite the characterization of human existence as worldly, temporal and historical, Heidegger has evaded the question of man's bodily existence. There is a predominance of man as *Da-sein* over man as a person living an earthly life. The phenomenon of body with its instincts and passions is left out of *Being and Time*. Indeed a phenomenological analysis worth its name should take into account a phenomenon like body. Body is a primordial phenomenon and there is nothing more phenomenal than the phenomenon of body in human existence. The absence of body is conspicuous in Heidegger's treatment of the world of intersubjectivity. Heidegger does refer to Dasein's Being with Others and to the various modes of the phenomenon of solicitude. But the treatment of Being-with and solicitude is without reference to body. All our expressions are primarily through the body. It is the body that mediates my relation with the Other. Body is the sole medium of communication with the Other. Concrete human relations are founded on the body, although the psyche too plays a role in them. Interpersonal relations, even the sublime ones, necessarily imply the existence of body. As a foremost phenomenologist, Heidegger is not justified in totally excluding the phenomenon of body from his analysis of human existence. Heidegger claims that his philosophy is not traditional and abstract but novel, concrete and time-bound. But a philosophy which does not deal with body cannot pass for a novel, concrete and temporal one.

And finally, Heidegger's notion of 'sight' is deficient in looking 'sideways.' That is why his treatment of intersubjectivity is very minimal and scanty. As it has already been mentioned above, Heidegger has given more importance to equipmental world than to communal world. The average everyday Dasein is shown to be existentially related to things. Dasein is related to persons only through the medium of things. Dasein is primarily a 'worker' in its concrete dealings with the environmental world. To Heidegger our everyday encounter with the Other is mostly inauthentic. He regards Dasein's existence in the public world as superficial and equates it with an anonymous 'they' (*das Man*). He hardly makes a mention of any genuine reciprocal relationship of give and take between Daseins. Moreover, he contents himself with the mention of the negative relation of indifference with the Other. Even the relation of solicitude is condemned to its everyday averageness of inauthenticity. This conspicuous neglect of authentic human relations is not accidental but intrinsic to Heidegger's thought. Authenticity is possible in the privacy of introspection. It is in 'loneliness' that one can understand and authenticate oneself. But Heidegger's Dasein is inalienably a Being-with-others. It is predominantly a Being determined by the 'they.' There is hardly any scope for Dasein to introspect and become authentic in relationship with the Other. Heidegger's treatment of Dasein's Being-with culminates itself in the truth of its finite, temporal Being. It is deprived of an adequate intersubjective dimension.

Another important deficiency of Heidegger's phenomenological ontology is that it lacks ethical dimension. Even his notion of authenticity is devoid of moral implications. Heidegger has not only avoided an attempt at a moral philosophy, he has even resented a moral interpretation of his phenomenological ontology. He has also ignored the ethical aspects of the history of Western metaphysics which he considered at length in his writings. He has exclusively focused his attention on the thinking of Being. He has considered man in terms of potentiality-to-be rather than in terms of ought-to-be. There is no place for the 'starry heavens above' and the 'moral law within' in Heidegger's treatment of Dasein. Since man is treated in terms of his belonging to Being, man is left without the *Other*, the Beyond, which may serve as the source of the Divine and the Ethical as well.

Besides the deficiencies in Heidegger's treatment of the notion of 'sight' there is ambiguity, rather ambivalence, in his twofold approach to the truth of Being. In the first phase of his thought he underlines freedom, a projection and resoluteness as the means of approaching the truth of Being. In the second phase, he regards resignation, receptivity and releasement as a way of approaching the meaning of Being. After the 'turn' in his thinking, Heidegger has not altogether abandoned his earlier position. He seems to have tried to maintain the two positions simultaneously. He has struggled to keep the validity of both the phases of his thought despite their incompatibility. He has not attempted at reconciling and bringing them together. He only swings the pendulum of his thought of Being between the two poles of his earlier and later positions. Heidegger is ambiguous in the interpretation of his two approaches to Being. He has not succeeded in throwing adequate light on the unity or the belonging-togetherness of the two stages of his thinking.

Ambiguity is not limited to his approach to the central question of the meaning of Being. It is prevalent even in his treatment of the related issues like everyday existence, disclosedness and nothingness. Heidegger is not clear whether everyday existence is identical with or different from inauthentic existence. He is not definite in determining the third constituent of disclosedness—is it discourse or falling? He is not decisive in his treatment of the notion of Nothing. There is confusion as to whether or not Nothing is identical with Being. So also the question of the Divine is most enigmatic of all in Heidegger. It is true that Heidegger is a profound thinker. Abstruseness and unintelligibility are bound to be there in such thinkers. But profundity should not be at the cost of clarity and distinctness.

The enigmatic and ambiguous character of Heidegger's philosophy is partly owing to his too much of dependence on German language. His attempts at extracting new meanings by adding prefixes and suffixes to the original terms have landed him in ambiguity. His attempts at exploiting the etymology of the German terms to suit his purpose have rendered his thought enigmatic. For instance, the term "Dasein" which is a combination of "Da" and "sein" does not lend itself to clear understanding. Its meaning is not only enigmatic but also ambiguous. Heidegger is of the firm view that German and Greek are the only languages that are suitable for philosophical thinking. This presupposition is not justifiable since there are other languages which are equally philosophical. Heidegger's knowledge of languages is limited to only a few languages of the West. He is not acquainted with the languages of the East like Sanskrit and Pali.

It may be said that Heidegger's phenomenological ontology presents a tragic picture of man and the world. It borders on nihilism since it lays too much of emphasis on radical finitude of Dasein. Death and Nothing permeate and dominate his thinking.

Man is made to move in a closed circle of Being-in-the-world of anxiety and emptiness. Man is cut away from the Other, the Divine. Death is the only all-dissolving end that man can await. Heidegger dwells at length on death, guilt and anxiety but pays little attention to feelings like friendship, loyalty and love. Fellow-feeling, cooperation and joy hardly find a mention. Man indeed is capable of genuine love for and commitment to the Other, the Divine. Of course, Heidegger regards Being as the substitute for the Divine. But the Being is enigmatic and he often equates it with Nothing.

Heidegger's analytic of Dasein is inadequate in the sense that it only deals with the ontological dimension of man to the neglect of other dimensions like social, political and economic. It fails to consider man within the practical framework. It does not deal with man's external life as expressed in political, social and economic experience which may be said to determine and reveal the ontological nature of man's existence. Heidegger regards ontological dimension of existence as revealing the primordial Being through which man becomes conscious of himself as existing. In this, Heidegger is under the impression that the ontological dimension alone constitutes the totality of human existence. Equating the whole of human existence with the ontological dimension at the expense of the other 'concrete' dimensions like the social, the political, the economic and the cultural renders Heidegger's ontology incomplete.

It may be argued that Heidegger 'destroyed' the whole of Western metaphysics from Plato to Hegel but without being able to establish a new, a better metaphysics in its place. Heidegger's metaphysics of Being cannot be regarded as a sound substitute for the metaphysics that precedes him. He was critical of traditional metaphysics as being *logos* centred and based on the essences. But devoid of logos and essence, Heidegger's metaphysics remains to be an empty metaphysics. It ceases to be a 'serious' and 'scientific' study of the reality. It is a study of reality more in terms of the natural dispositions of man than in terms of the logos and the logical essences of the reality itself.

It may also be contended that Heidegger's attempt at dealing with the question of the meaning of Being by dispensing with consciousness, thought or mind is unconvincing. No doubt, it is through the analytic of Dasein's existentialia that Being is 'constituted.' The structure of Being is founded in the being of Dasein, the privileged entity which is both ontic and ontological. But Heidegger constructs Being without analyzing Dasein as a being of consciousness. Since mind or thought is the central dimension of man, Heidegger should have founded his inquiry into Being on mind. Devoid of an adequate analysis of mind, Heidegger's interpretation of Being and Dasein seems to be more arbitrary than authentic.

As regards the method, it may be said that Heidegger is not a phenomenologist in the strict sense. According to Husserl, the pioneer of phenomenological method as a rigorous and radical science, phenomenology is essentially an intuition into the essences of the phenomenon of consciousness. Its aim is laying foundations of our knowledge of reality in our consciousness itself. It aims at discovering in our intentional consciousness certain categories which constitute the foundations of our knowledge of being. But Heidegger dispensed with this kind of phenomenology as being idealistic and narrow. He tried to broaden the foundations of the method and be more fundamental than his teacher. By broadening the range of the phenomena of his method, he tried to apprehend them through emotions, states-of-mind and moods, instead of intuitions or insights. Thus the foundation as well as the constitution of the Being of Dasein and Being in general is rather arbitrary and unconvincing. His metaphysics or ontology is more a natural disposition of man than a 'science.'

After having pointed out some inadequacies in Heidegger's thought, let us now turn to the merits of it. Critical appraisal can not stop with highlighting demerits. It is complete only when it brings to light the positive aspects as well. It is easier to point out the errors in the work of a great thinker than to show his valuable contributions. Heidegger himself says that 'he who thinks greatly must err greatly.' To him, an error is nothing but an exaggerated truth. And this is very much true in his case. Heidegger fixed his attention solely on the truth of Being. He spent all his philosophical energy in cutting his way towards Being. In working it out Heidegger had to exaggerate the question of the meaning of Being to the extent that he had to neglect some of other areas of human existence. Nevertheless Heidegger's exposition of Being through the Being of Dasein bears a testimony to his philosophical acumen and genius. His handling of the problematic of the meaning of Being is not only unique but also revolutionary.

Heidegger deplores the dismal condition of Western Philosophical tradition which preoccupied itself with 'conceptual' thinking of entities in their unity and universality. He is critical of Western metaphysics for not giving adequate attention to the coming-to-be of Being in the entities. Heidegger pioneered a metaphysics—fundamental ontology—which lets Being epochally present itself in the entities, especially in the entity called Dasein. It requires great courage, depth of understanding and originality to oppose the orthodox and monolithic structure of Western metaphysics. Heidegger's ontology, unlike Plato's metaphysics of the transcendental world of essences, is all-encompassing in its own way although it is exclusive of some popular themes. Heidegger was diligent and refused to be disturbed by the themes other than the truth of Being. He fixed his vision exclusively on interpreting the meaning of Being.

In our critical estimate of Heidegger's thought we held that he failed to take an upward theological and a downward 'earthly' look at human existence. We also held that his ontology lacks a moral dimension. But it may be held in defence of Heidegger that he is not an eclectic thinker to take all dimensions of human existence into consideration. Heidegger is a seminal and original thinker who concentrated on one thought, namely, the thought of the truth of Being. Indeed it is not possible for a creative genius like Heidegger to be multi-dimensional in his thought. Although one-dimensional, Heidegger's thought potentially contains other dimensions also. The theological, the moral, and the political dimensions are implied in Heidegger's ontology of Being. There is something 'unsaid' in what is said in his *Being and Time*.

We also pointed out that Heidegger neglected the question of intersubjectivity. But it may be held that Heidegger's concept of Being-with indeed provides a good basis for a philosophy of the Other. To Heidegger, other persons are not self-enclosed pure egos but encountered in the concrete world of Dasein. Dasein is essentially a being that exists with Others. Without Others, Dasein ceases to be Dasein. Authentic existence means being open to the Being of Others. Authentic self is that which includes intersubjectivity, environmentality, temporality and history. To be oneself presupposes to be with Others. Thus the intersubjective dimension is implicit in Heidegger's thought, although he has not worked it out fully.

This shows that Heidegger has chosen to deal with what is foundational to all other ways of thinking about human existence. The theological, the moral, the psychological and the political are included in his primordial approach to the truth of Being. The greatest virtue of Heidegger's philosophy is that it steers clear of the extremes like idealism and realism, theism and atheism, etc. The history of philosophy is an attempt to establish the primacy of the mind or the world and relate the subject and object which are claimed to be exclusive and independent realities. As regards the question of God, theists put forward categorical arguments and detailed descriptions about God, whereas atheists with their counter arguments unequivocally reject the existence of God. But Heidegger does not fall into either of the extremes of idealism or realism, theism or atheism. He altogether dispenses with the dogmatic approach of clinging to extremes. He adopts a middle path, a projective hermeneutical thinking, which bridges the subject-object dichotomy. Heidegger's primordial medial approach is neither practical nor theoretical, neither moral nor immoral, neither rational nor irrational. The projective hermeneutical thinking is founded on the realm that is fundamental to the extreme ways of thinking. It steers clear of the extreme forms of thinking by taking a step-back into primordiality.

Heidegger's ontology of radical finitude is not without significance. His notion of finitude is unique in the sense that it does not signify Dasein's end. As a being of finitude Dasein does not come to a stop but dwells as a being-in-the-world. Finitude marks the time-bound existence of Dasein. Heidegger's concept of finitude is an insight into the temporo-historical structure of human reality. It renders Heidegger's philosophy dynamic and open in contrast to the utopian philosophies which keep reality and its concepts in a timeless, unchanging and ideal realm of eternity. It is not proper to treat Heidegger's concept of finitude as the tragic doom of human existence. On the contrary, finitude speaks of the earthly existence wherein Dasein is resolutely receptive to the infinite number of possibilities. Through the notion of possibilities, Heidegger intends to awaken man to the finite truth of his given possibilities. He exposes man to the finite but concrete situation 'here and now' and the stark realities he encounters therein—thrownness, guilt, nothing, withdrawal, concealment, fear and anxiety. Heidegger's philosophy of finitude does not plunge man into triviality and absurdity. On the contrary, it lets man discover meaning and wholeness in a 'given' situation which is radically finite.

Another merit of Heidegger's philosophy is that it has a profound impact on religion, especially Christianity. Although Heidegger speaks very little of God, he has greatly influenced Christian theology. Besides theology, Heideggerian thinking has spread to other areas of thought like philosophical anthropology, philosophy of history, aesthetics, literature, hermeneutics and psychiatry. Heidegger's profundity has gone beyond academic circles and commands admiration even from non-professionals. The depth and dynamism of his thought is so conspicuous that even his critics find it hard to ignore. Heidegger's advent into philosophy is neither accidental nor transitory, but it is 'necessary' and lasting. Heidegger has come to give a much needed turn to Western metaphysics. And he has come to stay for generations to come.

The greatest contribution that Heidegger has made to philosophy and to the world of humanity at large is the belonging-togetherness of man and Being which is a home for the world-civilization and in which philosophical, cultural, religious and linguistic diversities are grounded and encompassed.

Bibliography

Alderman, Harold G., "Heidegger on Being Human." *Philosophy Today*, 15, 1971, pp. 16-29.

_____, "Heidegger: The Necessity and Structure of the Question of Being." *Philosophy Today*, 14, 1970, pp. 141-47.

Allen, E.L., *Existentialism from within*. Routledge & Kegan Paul, London, 1976.

Bailiff, John, D., *Coming to Be: An Interpretation of the Self in the Thought of Martin Heidegger*. University Microfilms, Ann Arbor, 1984.

Barrett, William, *Irrational Man—A Study in Existential Philosophy*. Heinemann, London, 1967.

Blackham, H.J. *Six Existentialist Thinkers*. Routledge & Kegan Paul, London, 1976.

Brown, James, *Kierkegaard, Heidegger, Buber and Barth: A Study of Subjectivity and Objectivity in Existential Thought*. Collier Books, New York, 1967.

Chatterjee, Margaret, *The Existential Outlook*. Orient Longman, New Delhi, 1973.

Collins, James, *The Existentialists—A Critical Study*. Henry Regery, Chicago, 1952.

Greene, Marjorie, *Existentialism—A Theory of Man*. Harvard University Press, Massachusetts, 1965.

Heidegger, Martin, *Being and Time*. Trans. John Macquarie & Edward Robinson, Basil Blackwell, Oxford, 1978.

_____, *The Basic Problems of Phenomenology*, Trans. and Intro. Albert Hofstadter, Indiana University Press, Bloomington, 1982.

_____, *Basic Writings*—Nine Key Essays, Plus the Introduction to *Being and Time*. Ed. with General Introduction and Introduction to Each Selection by David Farrell Krell, Routledge & Kegan Paul, London and Henley, 1978.

_____, *Discourse on Thinking*. Trans. John M. Anderson and E. Hans Freund Harper & Row, New York, 1966.

_____, *Early Greek Thinking*. Trans. David F. Krell and Frank A. Capuzzi, Harper & Row, New York, 1975.

_____, *The End of Philosophy*. Trans. Joan Stambaugh, Souvenir Press, London, 1975.

_____, *Existence and Being*. Introduced and analysed by Werner Brock, Gateway Edition, Indiana, 1967.

_____, *Identity and Difference*. Trans. Joan & Stambaugh, Harper Torchbook Edition, New York, 1974.

_____, *An Introduction to Metaphysics*. Trans. Ralph Manheim, Yale University Press, London-1959.

_____, *Kant and the Problem of Metaphysics*. Trans. Michael Heim, Indiana University Press, Bloomington, 1984.

_____, *The Question of Being*. Trans. William Kluback and Jean T. Wilde. College and University Press, New Haven, 1958.

_____, *What is Philosophy?* Trans. W. Kluback and J.T. Wilde, Twayne, Boston, 1958.

_____, *What is Called Thinking?* Trans. Glenn Gray. Harper & Row, New York, 1968.

_____, *The Question Concerning Technology and Other Essays*. Trans. William Lovitt. Harper & Row, New York, 1977.

_____, "Postscript," *Existentialism from Dostoevsky to Sartre*, ed. Walter Kaufmann, New American Library, New York, 1975, pp. 257-64.

Heinmann, F.H., *Existentialism and the Modern Predicament*. Harper, New York, 1958.

Kuhn, Helmut, *Encounter with Nothingness: An Essay on Existentialism*. The Humanist Library, Illinois, 1949.

Langan, Thomas, *The Meaning of Heidegger*. Columbia University Press, New York, 1959.

Lee, Edward N., & Mandelbaum, Mourice, ed. *Phenomenology and Existentialism*. The John Hopkins Press, Baltimore, 1967.

Macmurry, John, *Existentialism*. Penguin, England, 1978.

Natanson, Maurice, *Essays in Phenomenology*. University of Ed. California, The Hague, 1966.

Olson, Robert G., *Existentialism: An Introduction*. Dover, New York, 1962.

Puthenpurackal, Johnson J., *Heidegger through Authentic Totality to Total Authenticity: A Unitary Approach to his Thought in its two Phases*. Louvion Philosophical Studies 2, Leuven University Press, 1987.

Rintelen, Von J., *Beyond Existentialism.* Translated from German by Hilda Graef, George Allen & Unwin London, 1961.

Richardson, William, *Heidegger:Through Phenomenology to Thought.* 3rd Edition, Martinus Nijhoff, The Hague, 1974.

Sartre, Jean-Paul, *Existentialism and Humanism.* Trans. Philip Mairet, 9th Printing, Methuen, London 1970.

Salis, J., *The Concept of the World: A Study in Phenomenological Ontology of Martin Heidegger*. University Microfilms International, Michigan, 1977.

Spiegelberg, Herbert, *The Phenomenological Movement—A Historical Introduction*. 2 Vols. Martinus Nijhoff, The Hague, 1961.

Srinivasan, G., *The Existentialist Concepts and the Hindu Philosophical Systems*. Udayana Publications, Allahabad, 1967.

Thevenez, Pierre, *What is Phenomenology?* Ed. with an Introduction by James M. Edie and Preface by John Wild, Quadrangle Books, Chicago, 1962.

Wahl, Jean, *Philosophies of Existence—An Introduction to the Basic Thought of Kierkegaard, Heidegger, Jaspers, Marcel, Sartre*. Trans. F.M. Lory, Routledge & Kegan Paul, London, 1969.

Warnock, Mary, *Existentialism.* Oxford University Press, London, 1971.

[illegible] ... Dover, New York, [illegible]

[illegible] *Hodge* [illegible] ... *Approach* [illegible] ... Studies [illegible] ... Press, [illegible]

[illegible] Allen & Unwin [illegible]

[illegible] ... *Ideas* ... Indiana ... [illegible] ... 1972 [illegible]

[illegible] ... Methuen, London, 1980 [illegible]

[illegible]

[illegible]

[illegible]

[illegible] Tibetan [illegible] ... New York [illegible] ... Routledge & Kegan Paul, London [illegible]

[illegible] ... *Meditation* [illegible] ... New York [illegible]

[illegible] Robert [illegible] New York, [illegible]

[illegible]

[illegible] Allen & Unwin [illegible]

[illegible]

[illegible] Methuen, London [illegible]

[illegible]

[illegible]

[illegible]

[illegible]

[illegible]

[illegible] New York, [illegible]

[illegible]

[illegible] Allen & Unwin [illegible]

[illegible]

[illegible] Publishing [illegible]

[illegible]

[illegible] Theosophical [illegible]

[illegible]